Personal Empowerment Menu

for 21st Century Students

Christian LeButt

LeButt Publishing, LLC
Highland, MI

Printed in the United States of America

LeButt, Christian
Personal Empowerment Menu for 21st Century Students

Includes bibliographical references

Editing / Proofreading by Lynn DeGrande

ISBN 978-0-9882255-1-0

LeButt Publishing, LLC
PO Box 1268
Highland, MI 48357-1268

Table of Contents

Our Changing World and the Skills We Need

GLOBALIZATION:

OUTSOURCING AND OFFSHORING

Modern technology allows people from countries around the world to do jobs that Americans used to do. If you have an issue with your computer and call the manufacturer for help, you might talk to someone in a far away country. That person can use the Internet to take control of your computer to fix the problem. While this is a neat example of technology, it also shows that modern computers and the Internet have enabled people from all parts of the world to have access to jobs that Americans used to do. This transfer of work using the Internet and modern communication technologies is called **outsourcing**.

What else can be outsourced? Workers in foreign countries like India can perform tasks such as selling credit cards, supporting customers with banking problems, helping American troops with computer glitches, and taking reservations for restaurants anywhere in the world. In India, these jobs bring prestige and what is considered to be good pay. A company in the United States can outsource work to a place on the other side of the globe where wages and rent are less than one-fifth of the cost in Western capitals.[1] Even parts of doctors' jobs can be outsourced, such as reading CAT scan results.[2] The airplane manufacturer Boeing outsources some of its engineering to Russian engineers.[3]

Let's now consider the issue of **offshoring**. In this practice, businesses move manual labor / manufacturing to other countries like China. The results of offshoring are rather easy to see. Just go to a store and read product labels to see the places where many of the goods are made. We have all encountered products made from all parts of the world, including China. With certain items, it can be hard to find any that are made in the USA. Offshoring adds yet another example of displaced workers: factory workers, whose employment opportunities are affected by the global economy.

We have looked at some ways in which globalization can affect American physicians, engineers, accountants, service workers, and factory workers. Surely, you can imagine other examples.

If this new competition hasn't already caught your attention, note the following: the combined populations of China and India are over eight times larger than that of the United States.[4] If you consider what globalization (outsourcing and offshoring) has already done to the job market for Americans, imagine what it will be like when the immense populations of China, India, and other emerging economies develop the abilities to do even more of the jobs that our citizens are accustomed to doing. The workforce of the future must be prepared to compete for work with billions of people from around the world.

TECHNOLOGY AND AUTOMATION

Even if there was no competition from foreign countries, jobs in America would continue to change. One major force causing a significant transformation in the workplace is the increased use of **technology and**

---

[1] (Friedman, 2005, pages 15, 18, 23, and 24)
[2] (Friedman, 2005, page 16)
[3] (Friedman, 2005, pages 227-228)
[4] (The World Factbook - Country Comparison: Population, 2012)

automation to improve productivity. A simple example is the development of self-checkout systems in stores. This technological tool allows customers to scan their own products and pay their bill without a cashier. Instead of hiring enough people to check out all the customers, the store owner can hire a small number of people to oversee the self-checkout area. The technology creates a situation where fewer people are needed and the work is more technical.

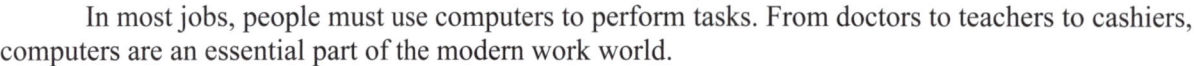

Automation has changed the face of the workplace. People in modern factories can now be seen working together with machines. As automation technology advances, the role of humans in factories decreases and changes.

In most jobs, people must use computers to perform tasks. From doctors to teachers to cashiers, computers are an essential part of the modern work world.

THE CHANGING WORKPLACE

Many of the middle class jobs in the last century could be done by workers who could learn processes or tasks and then repeat them. Factory workers needed to repeat tasks in the production of goods. Clerical workers and secretaries needed to learn basic processes and then repeat those processes. Cashiers needed to repeatedly apply basic math skills when dealing with customers. The problem in the new economy is that many of the learn-and-repeat jobs of the past are being lost to outsourcing, offshoring, technology, and automation. The types of occupations that are becoming available in the new century rely on a more advanced set of skills (even for those few people who will still work in factories or in such jobs as self-checkout monitors). The jobs that we will perform require more advanced critical thinking, creativity, collaboration, and people skills. Therefore, we must empower ourselves with 21st century skills. *This will be a new education for a new economy and a new world.*

THE SKILLS WE WILL NEED

What skills will we need in order to successfully meet the needs of employers, customers, clients, and patients in the future? Let's look at a recent study that surveyed over 400 employers in the United States. (*Are They Really Ready To Work: Employers' Perspectives on the Basic Knowledge and Applied Skills of New Entrants to the 21st Century U.S. Workforce,* retrieved from The Partnership for 21st Century Skills: www.p21.org) The survey showed that in order to have workplace success, new workers need to go beyond simply having a solid foundation of basic knowledge and skills in reading, writing, math, science, social studies, and language. They need "applied skills," which are the skills that allow a worker to apply his or her basic knowledge for practical purposes.[5] Also, Thomas Friedman researched the changing world economy and described the skills and attributes that he believes will lead to success in the future workforce in his book, *The World is Flat.*[6] The following list combines the skills that these sources determined are important for modern workers:

---

[5] (Casner-Lotto, 2006, pages 9 and 16)
[6] (Friedman, 2005, pages 281-309)

2

Job Skills, Attitudes, and Habits Needed in the 21st Century

- **Critical Thinking/Problem Solving** - Use sound reasoning and analytical thinking; use information to solve challenges; apply math and science concepts to problem solving.
- **Creativity/Innovation** - Display originality and inventiveness; integrate knowledge.
- **Communications** - Articulate well through speaking and writing.
- **Teamwork/Collaboration** - Collaborate with coworkers and customers; use teamwork; manage conflicts.
- **Diversity** - Work with people of all backgrounds.
- **Leadership** - Promote the strengths of others; coach and develop others.
- **Professionalism/Work Ethic** - Maintain accountability and effective work habits.
- **Ethics/Social Responsibility** - Maintain integrity and ethical behavior; act in community-minded ways.
- **Lifelong Learning/Self-Direction** - Learn new things; monitor own needs; learn from mistakes.
- **Information Technology Application** - Use technology to accomplish tasks and to problem-solve.[7]
  (Are They Really Ready To Work: Employers' Perspectives on the Basic Knowledge and Applied Skills of New Entrants to the 21st Century U.S. Workforce, retrieved from The Partnership for 21st Century Skills: www.p21.org)

- **Passion and Curiosity** - With these intrinsic qualities, become self-educators and self-motivators.
- **Adaptability and Versatility** - Have a deep set of skills over a range of topics in order to keep a job and also to find new work in a quickly changing work world.
- **Efficiency** - Leverage skills and tools to quickly solve problems and create efficient processes in order to out-compete cheaper foreign workers or new machines.
- **Explaining Skills** - Explain the complexities of a product or process in simple terms to coworkers, customers, clients, or patients.
- **Personalizing Skills** - Add a personal, human touch that cheaper foreign labor or machines might not be able to add.
- **"Green" Skills and Habits** - With rapidly growing economies in India, China, and the former Soviet Republics, the demand for resources and environmental jobs will grow.[8]
  (The World is Flat by Thomas Friedman)

These skills, attitudes, and habits used to be beneficial in the workplace and everyday life. Now, they are essential.

EMPOWERING OURSELVES

The sections of this book are designed to help you develop the skills, attitudes, and habits listed above and empower you for success in your future education, work, and personal life. Although the titles of the sections do not match the list above, these sections do address the skills, attitudes, and habits above.

In addition, the sections of this book will help you develop meaningful connections to your learning, future, teachers, parents, school, peers, community, and world. These connections will empower you in life and help you as you develop your skills inside and outside of school. University of Missouri researchers have shown the importance of connections. Their extensive survey of research shows that increased school attachment and relationships are associated with higher school achievement (including grades and standardized test scores), greater social and emotional success, improved behavior, and a greater willingness to work on challenging tasks.[9]

In all, the sections of this book will help you empower yourself with skills, attitudes, habits, and connections that will help you now and throughout life.

---

[7] (Casner-Lotto, 2006, pages 9 and 16)
[8] (Friedman, 2005, pages 281-309)
[9] (Bergin, 2009, page 141)

Connecting My Learning
to the Real World and Life

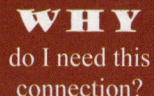 **WHY** do I need this connection?	To be successful in life, I will need to go beyond knowing facts and information. *I will need to understand how my knowledge is useful and be able to apply it for practical purposes in my career and personal life.* I need to understand the real-world value of the things I learn.
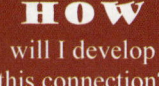 **HOW** will I develop this connection?	Below, there are some strategies (★) for developing connections between my learning and the real world and life. To help myself use these strategies, I will *ask* myself the ❓ Personal Empowerment Questions (PEQs) and strive to *answer* them.

★ **When learning new things, I will use the strategies below.**
❓ **I will ask Personal Empowerment Questions (PEQs) like those below and strive to answer them.**

ASKING INQUIRING QUESTIONS AND LOOKING FOR ANSWERS

❓ Why?
❓ How does ____ work?
❓ How did ____ come to be?
❓ Why do we ____?

❓ What are my predictions for ____?
❓ What do I already know about this?
❓ What do I need to know to get an answer?

CONNECTING NEW LEARNING TO EVERYDAY LIFE

❓ How does this relate to my life?
❓ Where have I encountered this before?

❓ Why does this matter to me?

PERFORMING REAL-LIFE (AUTHENTIC) TASKS WITH NEW LEARNING

❓ What can I do with this information or skill?
❓ How do people commonly make use of this knowledge or skill?
❓ How might I use this knowledge or skill in my future?

❓ What are my goals in doing ____?
❓ How can I accomplish ____?
❓ What steps, information, and procedures will allow me to do ____ in life?

DEVELOPING INSIGHTS AND OPINIONS ON REAL-WORLD ISSUES

❓ What do I believe about ____?
❓ How can I back up my opinion with facts?

❓ How might my opinion differ from other people's opinions and why?

IMAGINING THE FUTURE WORLD

❓ How will things be similar or different in the future?
❓ Given the current circumstances of ____, what could happen in the future?

❓ What will my life be like in the future?
❓ What do I want to see in the future?
❓ Wouldn't it be neat if ____ happens someday?

CONNECTING NEW LEARNING WITH PREVIOUSLY LEARNED KNOWLEDGE AND SKILLS

- How does this new knowledge or skill relate to what I already know?
- How does this new knowledge or skill deepen my understanding of ____?
- Is this new concept similar to or different from other concepts I know?
- With my new understanding, how can I use prior knowledge or skills in new ways?

FINDING CONNECTIONS AMONG SUBJECTS

- How do my knowledge and skills from one subject help me in another?
- How does this concept relate to other subjects?

CREATING PRODUCTS RELATED TO NEW LEARNING

- What am I trying to convey with my product?
- Who is my audience for this product?
- How can I demonstrate my understanding of ____ through the creation of a product?
- What can I produce with my understanding of ____?
- How can I be creative when making my product?

BECOMING NEW LEARNING

- What would it be like if I were the object, person, place, or process from my new learning?
- What can I learn by imagining myself as this object, person, place, or process?

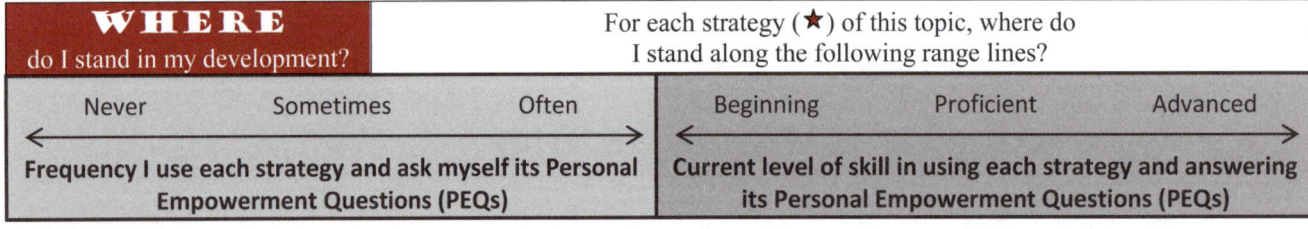

WHERE do I stand in my development?	For each strategy (★) of this topic, where do I stand along the following range lines?	
Never Sometimes Often	Beginning Proficient Advanced	
Frequency I use each strategy and ask myself its Personal Empowerment Questions (PEQs)	Current level of skill in using each strategy and answering its Personal Empowerment Questions (PEQs)	

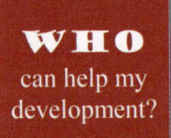

WHO can help my development?
- In addition to using the range-lines above for self-assessment, I can ask others (parents, teachers, mentors, and peers) to assess me so that I can learn and grow from their observations and input.
- I can observe the ways in which other people approach the skills I want to learn. What do other people do well? What do they need to improve? How can I use their example to improve myself?
- I can talk to other people about how they approach the skills I want to develop. I can ask what strategies they use to be successful.

Connecting with My Future and Career

WHY do I need this connection?	Changes in technologies and the economy of the world are rapidly shifting the types of jobs that will be available in the future. To be successful in my future, *I will need to understand these changes and understand which skills, attitudes, and habits will empower me to thrive in our new and changing work world. In addition, I should pursue interests and passions that could lead to future careers.*
HOW will I develop this connection?	Below, there are some strategies (★) for developing a connection with my possible future careers. To help myself use these strategies, I will *ask* myself the ❓ Personal Empowerment Questions (PEQs) and strive to *affirm* the • Personal Empowerment Statements (PESs).

★ **In school and everyday life, I will use the strategies below.**
❓ **I will ask Personal Empowerment Questions (PEQs) like those below.**
• **I will strive to affirm Personal Empowerment Statements (PESs) like those below.**

⭐ 1 LEARNING ABOUT THE NEW ECONOMY

❓ What types of careers were common in the past and how have they changed?

❓ What careers will grow in the future, and what careers will likely shrink?

❓ What are automation, offshoring, and outsourcing?

❓ With whom are we competing for work in the modern economy?

❓ How do technology and automation affect the workplace?

❓ Which jobs are more insulated from global competition and automation and which are not?

❓ With which people and technologies will I likely work in the future?

❓ Against which people and technologies will I likely compete in the future?

• I understand how the past economy is different from the future economy.

• I can achieve success in the future by developing knowledge and skills that are relevant to the modern economy and the careers in which I have an interest.

• I will work hard for success!

⭐ 2 LEARNING WHICH SKILLS, ATTITUDES, AND HABITS ARE NECESSARY FOR FUTURE SUCCESS

❓ Considering the rapid development of a global economy and technology, which skills will help me thrive in the 21st century?

❓ Which skills are especially important in my particular career field?

❓ In school, lessons teach me knowledge about various subjects. Why is it beneficial for these lessons to be taught in such a way that I develop critical thinking, problem solving, creativity, technological, or social skills?

❓ Beyond knowledge and skills, what personal attitudes and habits will help me succeed in the future?

❓ How and where can I learn more about the skills, habits, and attitudes I need for 21st century success?

❓ What are the strengths and weaknesses that I notice in the skills, attitudes, and habits of the people around me, and what can I learn from these people?

• I understand which skills, attitudes, and habits will help me thrive in the future, and I will strive to develop these traits.

• I will follow my interests with passion and curiosity.

7

DISCOVERING INTERESTS AND PASSIONS
THAT COULD LEAD TO FUTURE CAREERS

- ❓ What sparks my interest, curiosity, or passion?
- ❓ Which tasks do I really enjoy?
- ❓ Which tasks give me a sense of accomplishment, fulfillment, or empowerment?
- ❓ Considering my interests, what careers do I aspire to achieve?

- I will follow my interests with passion and curiosity.
- Through education, I can pursue my deepest interests.

WHERE do I stand in my development?	For each strategy (★) of this topic, where do I stand along the following range lines?	
Never Sometimes Often	Beginning Proficient Advanced	
Frequency I use each strategy, ask myself its Personal Empowerment Questions (PEQs), and affirm its Personal Empowerment Statements (PESs)	Current level of skill in using each strategy, answering its Personal Empowerment Questions (PEQs), and affirming its Personal Empowerment Statements (PESs)	

WHO can help my development?	• In addition to using the range-lines above for self-assessment, I can ask others (parents, teachers, mentors, and peers) to assess me so that I can learn and grow from their observations and input. • I can observe the ways in which other people approach the skills I want to learn. What do other people do well? What do they need to improve? How can I use their example to improve myself? • I can talk to other people about how they approach the skills I want to develop. I can ask what strategies they use to be successful.

Connecting with My Educators, Parents, and Future Mentors

WHY do I need this connection?	My teachers and parents are great sources for guiding my development and empowering me with the skills, habits, and attitudes that will help me thrive in the 21st century. In the future, I will have mentors in the workplace and in personal life who can help me succeed. *By developing connections with my current educators, parents, and future mentors, I help them to learn about me, understand who I am, communicate with me, mentor me, support me, motivate me, and help me develop into a successful and independent person.*
HOW will I develop this connection?	I will *ask* myself the ❓ Personal Empowerment Questions (PEQs) and strive to *affirm* the • Personal Empowerment Statements (PESs) below.

☆ **In school, the workplace, and everyday life, I will strive to make connections with my educators, parents, and mentors.**
❓ **I will ask Personal Empowerment Questions (PEQs) like those below.**
• **I will strive to affirm Personal Empowerment Statements (PESs) like those below.**

CONNECTING WITH EDUCATORS, PARENTS, AND MENTORS

❓ How do I promote mutual respect with my educators, parents, and mentors?
❓ How can I help my educators, parents, and mentors communicate with, connect with, understand, and mentor me?
❓ What connects me to my educators, parents, and mentors?

• I have quality relationships with my educators, parents, and mentors.

• My educators, parents, and mentors are real people who are passionate, fun, positive, humble, and trustworthy.
• My educators, parents, and mentors care about me, notice me, respect me, like me, believe in me, appreciate me, support me, trust me with responsibility, and help me.

WHERE do I stand in my development?	Where do I stand along the following range lines?
Never Sometimes Often ⟵————————————⟶ Frequency that I seek to develop connections with my educators, parents, and mentors; ask myself the Personal Empowerment Questions (PEQs); and affirm the Personal Empowerment Statements (PESs)	Beginning Proficient Advanced ⟵————————————⟶ Current level of success in connecting with my educators, parents, and mentors; answering the Personal Empowerment Questions (PEQs); and affirming the Personal Empowerment Statements (PESs)

WHO can help my development?	• In addition to using the range lines above for self-assessment, I can ask others (parents, teachers, mentors, and peers) to assess me so that I can learn and grow from their observations and input. • I can observe the ways in which other people approach the skills I want to learn. What do other people do well? What do they need to improve? How can I use their example to improve myself? • I can talk to other people about how they approach the skills I want to develop. I can ask what strategies they use to be successful.

9

Connecting with My Learning and Work Environments

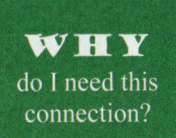**WHY** do I need this connection?	In my future career, a positive work environment will allow me and coworkers to succeed. In school, a quality learning environment allows me and other students to obtain knowledge and skills that will empower us to be successful. *For the success of all, I should do my part to responsibly support a quality learning environment. Not only will this help me learn now, it will teach me how to positively support my future work environment.*
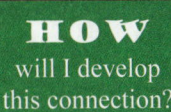**HOW** will I develop this connection?	Below, there are some strategies (★) for supporting a quality learning and work environment. To help myself use these strategies, I will *ask* myself the ❓ Personal Empowerment Questions (PEQs) and strive to *affirm* the • Personal Empowerment Statements (PESs).

★ **In school and in my future work environment, I will use the strategies below.**
❓ **I will ask Personal Empowerment Questions (PEQs) like those below.**
• **I will strive to affirm Personal Empowerment Statements (PESs) like those below.**

1 CREATING A WELCOMING ENVIRONMENT

❓ Why do I feel like I belong here?

• I feel welcome and important here.

• I want to promote a welcome feeling among others.

2 CREATING A SAFE ENVIRONMENT

❓ Why do I feel safe here?

• I and others behave respectfully here.

• I trust the people and physical structure around me.

3 CREATING A RESPONSIBLE ENVIRONMENT

❓ What are my responsibilities as a learner?
❓ What do I need to do in order to be successful?

• I plan for success, behave proactively, accept responsibility, and work hard.

4 CREATING A SUCCESSFUL ENVIRONMENT

❓ In what ways am I prepared to handle challenges?
❓ Am I being positive and seeing my own great potential?
❓ What can I do to improve my performance?

❓ In what ways am I building my success?
❓ How can I perform this task so that it feels manageable?

• I will succeed!

CREATING A DISTRACTION-FREE ENVIRONMENT

- ❓ How can I positively affect the learning environment?
- ❓ How can I avoid creating distractions for others?

- I am a focused, good citizen who does not distract others.

CREATING A GOAL-ORIENTED ENVIRONMENT

- ❓ What are my dreams for the future?
- ❓ What goals do I need to achieve in order to reach my dreams?
- ❓ To what degree am I meeting my goals?
- ❓ What things am I doing well?
- ❓ What do I need to improve?

- ❓ What steps can I take to better achieve my goals?

- I will accomplish my dreams, because I set goals and follow a plan for success.

CREATING AN EMPOWERING ENVIRONMENT

- ❓ How would I like to demonstrate my understanding, learn a concept, or extend my knowledge of a concept?
- ❓ In what ways am I empowered to achieve my goals for the future and the present?
- ❓ How can I achieve self-reliance?

- ❓ In what ways are my school experiences preparing me for my future?

- I will have future success, because I am empowering myself through positive educational choices.

CREATING A TEAM-ORIENTED ENVIRONMENT

- ❓ How can we support one another in building success?
- ❓ How can I contribute to our success as a team?
- ❓ How can I promote positive group interactions?

- I am a supportive and positive member of the team.

CREATING A FUN AND EXCITING ENVIRONMENT

- ❓ Why is school enjoyable, and how do I support this?

- School is fun, exciting, and interesting! I love it!

CREATING A TECHNOLOGICAL ENVIRONMENT

- ❓ Why do I like these technological learning tools?

- This technology suits the ways in which my generation thinks and creates.

- This technology is useful for real-world purposes such as _____.

CREATING A CURIOUS ENVIRONMENT

❓ Why?
❓ How did that come to be?
❓ How does that work?

❓ How can I do _____?

• I want answers to interesting questions.

 ## CREATING A VISUALLY PLEASING ENVIRONMENT

❓ Why am I comfortable here?

• I enjoy and support surroundings that are clean, well-maintained, attractive, and inspiring.

 ## CREATING A DISCIPLINED ENVIRONMENT

❓ How do I support the system of discipline in this classroom?

• I want a positive learning environment so that I can succeed, and my teacher's discipline system supports this goal.

• I see the value of my teacher's discipline system.
• My educator is reasonable, fair, and trustworthy.
• I feel respected here.

WHERE do I stand in my development?	For each strategy (★) of this topic, where do I stand along the following range lines?	
Never Sometimes Often ←——————————————→	Beginning Proficient Advanced ←——————————————→	
Frequency I use each strategy, ask myself its Personal Empowerment Questions (PEQs), and affirm its Personal Empowerment Statements (PESs)	Current level of skill in using each strategy, answering its Personal Empowerment Questions (PEQs) and affirming its Personal Empowerment Statements (PESs)	

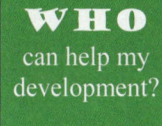

WHO can help my development?	• In addition to using the range lines above for self-assessment, I can ask others (parents, teachers, mentors, and peers) to assess me so that I can learn and grow from their observations and input. • I can observe the ways in which other people approach the skills I want to learn. What do other people do well? What do they need to improve? How can I use their example to improve myself? • I can talk to other people about how they approach the skills I want to develop. I can ask what strategies they use to be successful.

Connecting with My Peers

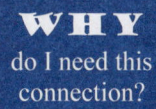 **WHY** do I need this connection?	Throughout my life, I will need to interact and work with others. By building positive relationships with peers, we will support and motivate each other in learning, work, and personal situations. *I should strive to meet new people and develop relationships that are mutually supportive.*
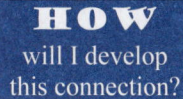 **HOW** will I develop this connection?	I will *ask* myself the ❓ Personal Empowerment Questions (PEQs) and strive to *affirm* the • Personal Empowerment Statements (PESs) below.

★ **In school, the workplace, and everyday life, I will strive to make connections with peers.**
❓ **I will ask Personal Empowerment Questions (PEQs) like those below.**
• **I will strive to affirm Personal Empowerment Statements (PESs) like those below.**

CONNECTING WITH PEERS

❓ How am I connecting with those around me?
❓ How can I become more engaged with my peers?
❓ How can I meet new people?
❓ How can I develop relationships?
❓ What can I learn from others?
❓ Which extracurricular activities grab my interest?

• I am meeting new people and developing deeper connections and relationships over time.
• I am involved and connected with people and activities outside of the classroom.

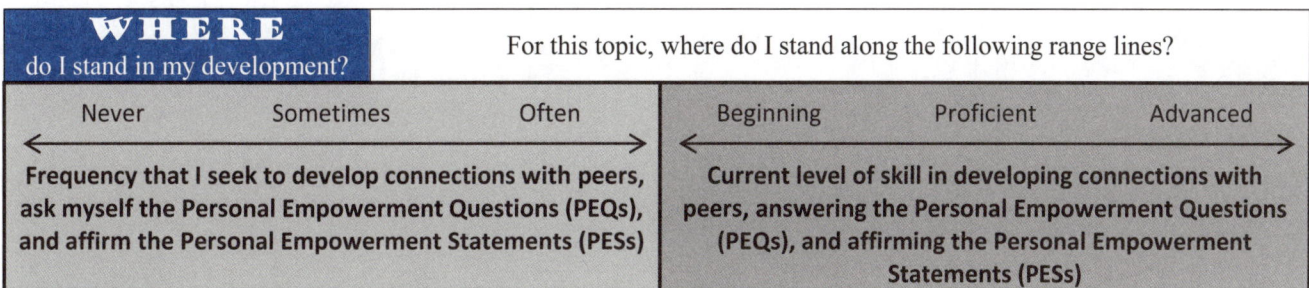

WHERE do I stand in my development?	For this topic, where do I stand along the following range lines?	
Never Sometimes Often	Beginning Proficient Advanced	
Frequency that I seek to develop connections with peers, ask myself the Personal Empowerment Questions (PEQs), and affirm the Personal Empowerment Statements (PESs)	Current level of skill in developing connections with peers, answering the Personal Empowerment Questions (PEQs), and affirming the Personal Empowerment Statements (PESs)	

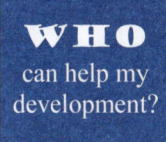 **WHO** can help my development?	• In addition to using the range lines above for self-assessment, I can ask others (parents, teachers, mentors, and peers) to assess me so that I can learn and grow from their observations and input. • I can observe the ways in which other people approach the skills I want to learn. What do other people do well? What do they need to improve? How can I use their example to improve myself? • I can talk to other people about how they approach the skills I want to develop. I can ask what strategies they use to be successful.

15

Connecting with the Spirit of My Teams

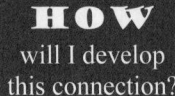**WHY** do I need this connection?	In my life, I am and will be a member of a number of competitive and noncompetitive teams. These will include my family; my work group; my school; and any teams, clubs, or organizations I choose to join. *These teams will all function more successfully if they are filled with a sense of team spirit. I should strive to embrace and promote a sense of team spirit in my family, my workplace, my school, and my other teams.*
HOW will I develop this connection?	Below, there are some strategies (★) for developing a connection with team spirit. To help myself use these strategies, I will *ask* myself the ❓ Personal Empowerment Questions (PEQs) and strive to *affirm* the • Personal Empowerment Statements (PESs).

★ In school, the workplace, and everyday team life, I will use the strategies below.
❓ I will ask Personal Empowerment Questions (PEQs) like those below.
• I will strive to affirm Personal Empowerment Statements (PESs) like those below.

CREATING A TEAM FEELING

❓ What makes me proud of my school and my other teams?

• I am a proud member of this amazing team.

PROMOTING PARTICIPATION IN ACTIVITIES

❓ How can I become more involved in my school and other teams?
❓ How can I encourage peers to participate in activities?

❓ How can I support my peers in their activities?

• I am a supportive member of school and team activities, and I try to get other people involved.

MAKING TEAM SUCCESS A BIG DEAL

❓ What gives me a sense of school and team spirit?
❓ What successes have my school and my team experienced?

• I am proud of my school and my team.

• This is a good school and team with successful people.
• A success for any one of us is a success for our whole school and team community.

CREATING ACTIVITIES TO PROMOTE SCHOOL AND TEAM SPIRIT

❓ What activities can I help develop that give people a sense of school spirit?

• I enjoy participating in the creation of spirit-related activities.

SEEING THE SPIRIT OF MY TEACHERS AND LEADERS

❓ How do my teachers and other leaders give me a sense of school and team spirit?

• My teachers and leaders love this school or team.

• My teachers and leaders care about us and support those things that are important to us.
• My teachers and leaders are proud members of the team.

17

★ TAKING A LEADERSHIP ROLE IN PROMOTING TEAM SPIRIT
6

- ❓ How can I promote school and team spirit and pride?
- ❓ How can I emulate the school and team spirit and pride of others?

- I am a leader in promoting school and team pride.

★ CREATING A PHYSICAL ENVIRONMENT
7 THAT STIMULATES SPIRIT

- ❓ How does the school or team environment increase my spirit?
- ❓ How can I contribute to a spirited physical environment?

- The things that I see as I walk around make me proud of my school or team and fill me with spirit.

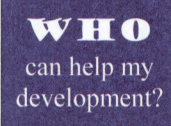

WHERE do I stand in my development?	For each strategy (★) of this topic, where do I stand along the following range lines?	
Never Sometimes Often	Beginning Proficient Advanced	
Frequency I use each strategy, ask myself its Personal Empowerment Questions (PEQs), and affirm its Personal Empowerment Statements (PESs)	**Current level of skill in using each strategy, answering its Personal Empowerment Questions (PEQs), and affirming its Personal Empowerment Statements (PESs)**	

WHO can help my development?	• In addition to using the range lines above for self-assessment, I can ask others (parents, teachers, mentors, and peers) to assess me so that I can learn and grow from their observations and input. • I can observe the ways in which other people approach the skills I want to learn. What do other people do well? What do they need to improve? How can I use their example to improve myself? • I can talk to other people about how they approach the skills I want to develop. I can ask what strategies they use to be successful.

Connecting with the Spirit of My Teams

Connecting with My Community

WHY do I need this connection?	My community includes a number of citizens who can serve as mentors in my development. Additionally, I can lend a hand to members of my community.[10] *I should strive to make community connections that can support my development and allow me to be an involved citizen.*
HOW will I develop this connection?	Below, there are some strategies (★) for developing connections with my community. To help myself use these strategies, I will *ask* myself the ❓ Personal Empowerment Questions (PEQs) and strive to *affirm* the • Personal Empowerment Statements (PESs).

★ **In school, the workplace, and everyday life, I will use the strategies below.**
❓ **I will ask Personal Empowerment Questions (PEQs) like those below.**
• **I will strive to affirm Personal Empowerment Statements (PESs) like those below.**

USING COMMUNITY MEMBERS AS MENTORS AND TEACHERS

❓ What can I learn from the members of my community?

❓ How can my community serve as a source of inspiration and a tool for my personal development?

❓ How can I use community resources to learn about possible career options?

- Through community members and resources, I am learning a great deal about life and about career options.
- My community inspires me.

SERVING THE COMMUNITY

❓ How are the knowledge and skills I learn relevant to my community?

❓ What issues face the members of my community?

❓ How can I positively help, support, and work with the members of my community?

❓ How can I help or start a charitable organization?

- School lessons and activities allow me to positively impact my community.
- I can make a difference.

WHERE do I stand in my development?	For each strategy (★) of this topic, where do I stand along the following range lines?
Never Sometimes Often ⟷ **Frequency I use each strategy, ask myself its Personal Empowerment Questions (PEQs), and affirm its Personal Empowerment Statements (PESs)**	Beginning Proficient Advanced ⟷ **Current level of skill in using each strategy, answering its Personal Empowerment Questions (PEQs), and affirming its Personal Empowerment Statements (PESs)**

---

[10] (ETR Associates, 2012)

WHO can help my development?	• In addition to using the range lines above for self-assessment, I can ask others (parents, teachers, mentors, and peers) to assess me so that I can learn and grow from their observations and input. • I can observe the ways in which other people approach the skills I want to learn. What do other people do well? What do they need to improve? How can I use their example to improve myself? • I can talk to other people about how they approach the skills I want to develop. I can ask what strategies they use to be successful.

Connecting with the World

WHY do I need this connection?	In the modern world, people can work in jobs that involve others from many different countries.[11] In the future, I might interact with people from other countries in my work or personal life. *To be effective, I should learn to understand the wants, needs, cultures, and values of people from various places. In addition, I should learn to communicate with people in other countries.*
HOW will I develop this connection?	Below, there are some strategies (★) for developing a connection with the world. To help myself use these strategies, I will *ask* myself the ❓ Personal Empowerment Questions (PEQs) and strive to *affirm* the • Personal Empowerment Statements (PESs).

★ In school, the workplace, and everyday life, I will use the strategies below.
❓ I will ask Personal Empowerment Questions (PEQs) like those below.
• I will strive to affirm Personal Empowerment Statements (PESs) like those below.

LEARNING THE WANTS, NEEDS, CULTURES, HISTORIES, AND VALUES OF OTHERS

❓ What are the values, religions, resources, needs, and wants of various people in countries around the world, and how are these things interrelated?

• With my understanding of people around the world, I can better work with others and generate products and services in a global economy.

LEARNING TO COMMUNICATE GLOBALLY

❓ What can I do to effectively communicate with people from other countries and cultures?
❓ What are the similarities and differences among world cultures?

• With an understanding of language, social norms, and culture, I can communicate with people from other parts of the world.

WHERE do I stand in my development?	For each strategy (★) of this topic, where do I stand along the following range lines?	
Never Sometimes Often ⟵————————————————⟶ **Frequency I use each strategy, ask myself its Personal Empowerment Questions (PEQs), and affirm its Personal Empowerment Statements (PESs)**	Beginning Proficient Advanced ⟵————————————————⟶ **Current level of skill in using each strategy, answering its Personal Empowerment Questions (PEQs), and affirming its Personal Empowerment Statements (PESs)**	

WHO can help my development?	• In addition to using the range lines above for self-assessment, I can ask others (parents, teachers, mentors, and peers) to assess me so that I can learn and grow from their observations and input. • I can observe the ways in which other people approach the skills I want to learn. What do other people do well? What do they need to improve? How can I use their example to improve myself? • I can talk to other people about how they approach the skills I want to develop. I can ask what strategies they use to be successful.

Connecting with the World

---
[11] (Friedman, 2005, page 243)

21

Thinking Critically

- I am *thinking critically* when I use one of these <u>specific analytical skills</u>:
- I am also *thinking critically* when I combine <u>specific analytical skills</u> (to the left) to make one of these more <u>complex assessments</u>:

WHAT is critical thinking?

Specific Analytical Skills
1. **Making Observations and Inferences**
2. **Comparing and Contrasting**
3. **Grouping and Categorizing**
4. **Understanding Cause and Effect**
5. **Understanding Sequence and Timing**
6. **Understanding the Big Picture**
7. **Identifying Patterns**

Complex Assessment Skills
1. **Assessing Accuracy, Validity, or Logic (Informational Literacy)**
2. **Assessing the Workings of Processes, Events, Strategies, and Solutions**
3. **Self-Assessing**
4. **Identifying and Predicting Problems**

WHY do I need critical thinking skills?

In my work, personal life, and education, I will need to think critically to analyze situations, processes, or problems. Only with this ability can I effectively perform tasks and solve problems. *I should develop my critical thinking skills so that I am empowered to understand and work through the challenges and tasks I encounter.* (Critical thinking requires analyzing and evaluating skills which are considered higher level thinking skills.[12])

HOW will I develop critical thinking skills?

Below, there are some critical thinking skills (☆). To help myself develop these skills, I will *ask* myself the ❓ Personal Empowerment Questions (PEQs) and strive to *answer* them.

☆ In school, the workplace, and everyday life, I will use the critical thinking skills below.
❓ To use and develop each skill, I will ask Personal Empowerment Questions (PEQs) like those below and strive to answer them.

Specific Analytical Skills

MAKING OBSERVATIONS AND INFERENCES

❓ What do I know about this object, challenge, situation, person, event, process, or action?

❓ What do I not know about this?

❓ What can I reasonably infer about this object, challenge, situation, person, event, process, or action?

COMPARING AND CONTRASTING

❓ Considering the characteristics I observe, what similarities and differences do I notice in these objects, challenges, situations, people, events, processes, or actions?

❓ Are the differences I notice large or small?

---
[12] (Anderson, 2001, pages 5 and 28)

23

GROUPING AND CATEGORIZING

- ❓ What groupings make the most sense based on similarities and differences?
- ❓ Why does this item go into one particular group as opposed to another group?
- ❓ What types of groups would other people likely make?
- ❓ How does organizing these things help me accomplish my goals?
- ❓ Will this organization work better or worse if organized in a different way?

UNDERSTANDING CAUSE AND EFFECT

- ❓ Why did that happen?
- ❓ What is the root cause of this problem?
- ❓ What do I expect to happen next?
- ❓ If this happens, then what will occur?
- ❓ What if this detail or relationship had been different?
- ❓ What problems might arise as a result of this action or event?
- ❓ Does this cause-and-effect relationship make sense?
- ❓ Will this strategy or solution work?

UNDERSTANDING SEQUENCE AND TIMING

- ❓ What if ____ had happened before ____?
- ❓ What if ____ had happened a little sooner or a little later?
- ❓ What is or would have been the best order for the steps of ____ to occur?
- ❓ When would be the best time to do ____?

UNDERSTANDING THE BIG PICTURE

- ❓ What is the overall meaning of these small details?
- ❓ What is the theme of these ideas or facts?
- ❓ What role does ____ play in the big picture?
- ❓ Why is ____ important in solving this problem?
- ❓ What details should be addressed to improve the overall picture?
- ❓ How would the big picture be different if ____ were removed or changed?

IDENTIFYING PATTERNS

- ❓ What seems to be repeating itself here?
- ❓ How is this pattern different from others?
- ❓ What seems to be recurring among these ____?
- ❓ What patterns seem to work or not work when applied to various situations?

Complex Assessment Skills

ASSESSING ACCURACY, VALIDITY, OR LOGIC

- ❓ What background information do I need to make this assessment?
- ❓ What assumptions are being made?
- ❓ How do they know that?
- ❓ Do the steps of this solution, argument, or experiment follow a logical path?
- ❓ Are there possible biases in this claim or opinion?
- ❓ What background information and facts back up this information, assumption, theory, or opinion?
- ❓ What do I need to understand in order to make a quality assessment?
- ❓ Would this be the same in all situations?
- ❓ What is the truth?
- ❓ Did this person or group making a claim follow the scientific method?

ASSESSING THE WORKINGS OF PROCESSES OR EVENTS

- ❓ How does this process, event, strategy, or solution work?
- ❓ Why is _____ happening?
- ❓ Is this what is supposed to happen?
- ❓ How does that person do _____ so well?
- ❓ Why is this process, event, strategy, or solution better than that one?

- ❓ What are the strengths and weaknesses of this process, event, strategy, or solution?
- ❓ Is there something in this process, event, strategy, or solution that could be improved?
- ❓ How would I prioritize these things?

SELF-ASSESSING

- ❓ What are my goals?
- ❓ Am I on track to meet my goals?
- ❓ What are my strengths and weaknesses?
- ❓ What is my role within this group or organization?
- ❓ What can I do to be better?
- ❓ What new skills and knowledge would help me in doing _____?

- ❓ What did I just learn from that activity?
- ❓ How does my opinion or feeling differ from others?
- ❓ Why is this hard or easy for me to do?
- ❓ How can I improve?
- ❓ What can I learn about myself by observing others?

IDENTIFYING AND PREDICTING PROBLEMS

- ❓ Based on everything I see here, what is the problem?
- ❓ What went wrong in this situation, event, procedure, solution, or action?
- ❓ What is the root cause of this challenge or issue?

- ❓ What are we trying to solve or fix?
- ❓ What problems might arise in this situation?
- ❓ What challenges could this solution create?

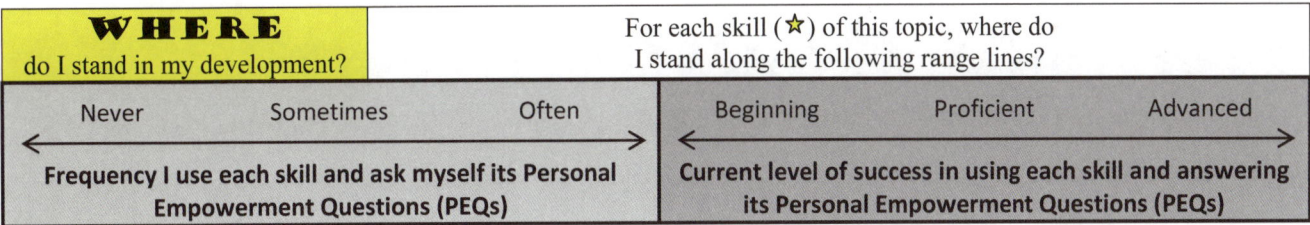

WHERE do I stand in my development?	For each skill (★) of this topic, where do I stand along the following range lines?	
Never Sometimes Often	Beginning Proficient Advanced	
Frequency I use each skill and ask myself its Personal Empowerment Questions (PEQs)	Current level of success in using each skill and answering its Personal Empowerment Questions (PEQs)	

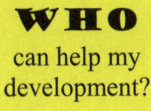 **WHO** can help my development?	• In addition to using the range lines above for self-assessment, I can ask others (parents, teachers, mentors, and peers) to assess me so that I can learn and grow from their observations and input. • I can observe the ways in which other people approach the skills I want to learn. What do other people do well? What do they need to improve? How can I use their example to improve myself? • I can talk to other people about how they approach the skills I want to develop. I can ask what strategies they use to be successful.

25

Taking Actions (like Solving Problems)

WHY do I need this skill?	Workers regularly plan and take actions (like solving problems). For example, doctors plan and carry out actions to make people healthier, engineers design bridges or other structures, teachers create and use lessons to educate students, or entrepreneurs develop and use methods to attract customers. In personal life, people plan family budgets and take steps to follow them or develop methods to communicate positively with others. *In my career and personal life, I will need to take real actions including ... solving problems, designing processes and strategies for accomplishing goals, expressing and promoting my opinions, etc.* (Taking action requires analyzing and evaluating skills which are considered higher level thinking skills.[13])
HOW will I develop this skill?	Below, there are some *basic steps that I should follow when taking any type of action*, from solving a problem to creating a process to writing a paper. To develop the ability to use these steps, I will strive to perform the procedures (bulleted within each step). To help myself do this, I will *ask* myself the ❓ Personal Empowerment Questions (PEQs) for each step and strive to *answer* them.

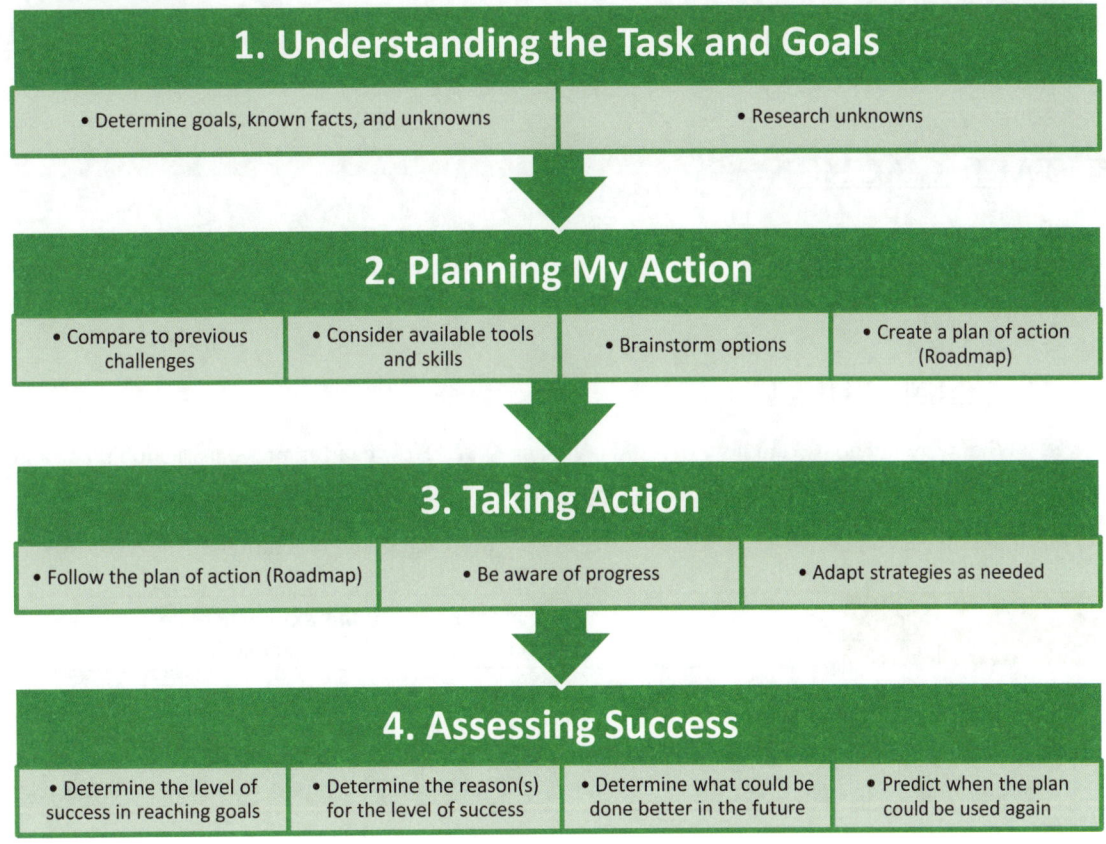

1. Understanding the Task and Goals

- Determine goals, known facts, and unknowns
- Research unknowns

2. Planning My Action

- Compare to previous challenges
- Consider available tools and skills
- Brainstorm options
- Create a plan of action (Roadmap)

3. Taking Action

- Follow the plan of action (Roadmap)
- Be aware of progress
- Adapt strategies as needed

4. Assessing Success

- Determine the level of success in reaching goals
- Determine the reason(s) for the level of success
- Determine what could be done better in the future
- Predict when the plan could be used again

★ In school, the workplace, and everyday life, I will follow the steps above and use the procedures within each step.
❓ To use each step and the procedures within it, I will ask Personal Empowerment Questions (PEQs) like the following and strive to answer them.

---

[13] (Anderson, 2001, pages 5 and 28)

UNDERSTANDING THE TASK AND GOALS

- ❓ What am I trying to figure out, prove, or develop?
- ❓ What are my goals in this problem or task?
- ❓ What information is given or is available?
- ❓ What clues are relevant?

- ❓ What information do I need, but do not have?
- ❓ What do I need to find out in order to solve this problem or complete this task?
- ❓ What do I already know about addressing this type of problem or task?

PLANNING MY ACTION

- ❓ What are my goals in this task?
- ❓ Considering the goals and information I have, what do I need to do?
- ❓ What tools do I have at my disposal?
- ❓ Is this similar to another task I've done?
- ❓ Do I already know a strategy for doing this task?
- ❓ Can I modify or combine strategies I've used for other tasks to do this one?
- ❓ Can I invent a new strategy to accomplish this task?

- ❓ Does someone else have another idea about how to do this?
- ❓ Considering my options, which strategy best accomplishes my goals?
- ❓ Considering my options, which strategy works best for my skill set?
- ❓ What is my plan (roadmap)?

TAKING ACTION

- ❓ What are my goals, and how does my action plan help me achieve these goals?
- ❓ Am I following my action plan (roadmap)?

- ❓ Where am I in my progression through this task?
- ❓ Do I need to adjust my plan in any way to better reach my goals?

ASSESSING SUCCESS

- ❓ What were my goals, and how well did my plan of action work?
- ❓ Why did certain strategies work well, and why did other strategies not work well?

- ❓ How can I improve my action plans and methods in the future?
- ❓ When might I be able to use these strategies again in the future?

WHERE do I stand in my development?	For each step (★) of this skill, where do I stand along the following range lines?	
Never　　　Sometimes　　　Often ⟷ **Frequency I use these steps and ask myself the Personal Empowerment Questions (PEQs)**	Beginning　　　Proficient　　　Advanced ⟷ **Current level of skill in using the steps and answering the Personal Empowerment Questions (PEQs)**	

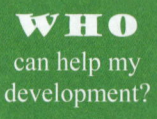

WHO can help my development?	• In addition to using the range lines above for self-assessment, I can ask others (parents, teachers, mentors, and peers) to assess me so that I can learn and grow from their observations and input. • I can observe the ways in which other people approach the skills I want to learn. What do other people do well? What do they need to improve? How can I use their example to improve myself? • I can talk to other people about how they approach the skills I want to develop. I can ask what strategies they use to be successful.

Being Creative

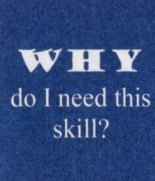 **WHY** do I need this skill?	In the new economy, being creative and innovative gives me a huge advantage in competing with other people. As new machines and computers are developed to perform tasks that humans used to do, creativity allows me to be more valuable to employers. *I should develop my creative skills so that I can excel in my career, doing such things as promoting a product or service, creating a new product or service, competing with other people or technologies, developing more efficient ways to perform tasks, etc. I will also gain benefits as my creativity helps me in my personal life.* (Creative skills are considered higher level thinking skills.[14])
HOW will I develop this skill?	Below, there are some strategies (★) for developing my creative skills. To help myself use these strategies, I will *ask* myself the ❓ Personal Empowerment Questions (PEQs) listed with each strategy and strive to *answer* them.

★ **In school, the workplace, and everyday life, I will use the strategies below.**
❓ **I will ask Personal Empowerment Questions (PEQs) like those below and strive to answer them.**

 ## DEVELOPING MY CREATIVE THINKING
(The following exercises can train creative thinking in my mind.)

 ## MAKING CONNECTIONS
(AMONG IDEAS, TOOLS, OBJECTS, EVENTS, PROCESSES, AND SKILLS)

❓ How are these things related?
❓ How does this relate to what I already know (my prior knowledge)?

❓ How can these things be connected to create useful new ideas, tools, objects, events, processes, skills, facts, strategies, and goals?

 ## SHIFTING PERSPECTIVES

❓ How would someone else interpret or view this ____?

❓ How does my perception of this ____ change by considering someone else's point of view?

 ## WITH A TOOL, OBJECT, PROCESS, OR SKILL IN MIND … IMAGINING NEW USES OR GOALS TO ACHIEVE

❓ What qualities does this tool, object, process, or skill possess?
❓ Does this tool, object, process, or skill remind me of something else?

❓ What else could I do with this tool, object, process, or skill?

 ## WITH A GOAL IN MIND … MANIPULATING CURRENT TOOLS, OBJECTS, PROCESSES, OR SKILLS TO ACHIEVE THE GOAL (SCAMPER)

❓ What tools, objects, processes, or skills are already available?
❓ In order to achieve my goals, what can I …

- **S**ubstitute?
- **C**ombine?
- **A**dapt?
- **M**odify / Magnify / Minify?

- **P**ut to other uses?
- **E**liminate?
- **R**everse / Rearrange?

(**SCAMPER**)[15]

---

[14] (Anderson, 2001, pages 5 and 28)
[15] (Eberle, 1996, page 6)

29

WITH A GOAL IN MIND … IMAGINING NEW AND UNUSUAL TOOLS, OBJECTS, PROCESSES, OR SKILLS TO ACHIEVE THE GOAL

- ❓ What is my goal?
- ❓ What plan of action would seem "wacky" at first thought?
- ❓ What way of doing this would I create in order to sound funny?
- ❓ What is the last thing I would normally think of when trying to _____?
- ❓ If I ignore reality for a moment, how would I do this task? After I think of some outrageous ideas, can I create new objects, tools, skills, or processes to make it work?

 DREAMING OF NEW CIRCUMSTANCES, NEW CAPABILITIES, AND NEW GOALS

- ❓ What would I love to see happen?
- ❓ Wouldn't it be awesome if _____ happened?
- ❓ What would I love to do or accomplish someday?

 **DETERMINING MY BEST IDEAS**

Questions to use when creating new ideas:
- ❓ Which idea or solution is most likely to achieve my goals?
- ❓ Which criteria need to be considered in picking out my best ideas?
- ❓ What is likely to go right or wrong if I use any of my ideas?

Questions to use after implementing new ideas:
- ❓ What did I hope my idea or solution would accomplish?
- ❓ Did I achieve my goals?
- ❓ What worked well?
- ❓ What didn't work well?
- ❓ What should I continue to do?
- ❓ What can I change?

 **FINDING AND USING OPPORTUNITIES TO BE CREATIVE**

(The following questions can help me find creative outlets.)

- ❓ Which activities allow me to think independently and make decisions?
- ❓ Where can I find open-ended opportunities to design something?
- ❓ Which school projects and assessments allow me to creatively display my understanding and skills?
- ❓ What creative uses can I imagine for the knowledge and skills I learn?
- ❓ What creative stories can I imagine that deal with new things that I learn?
- ❓ What challenges and problems can I create to solve?
- ❓ What creative ways can I generate for remembering new learning?
- ❓ Considering what I know, what are the best and worst ways that I can imagine for doing a task?

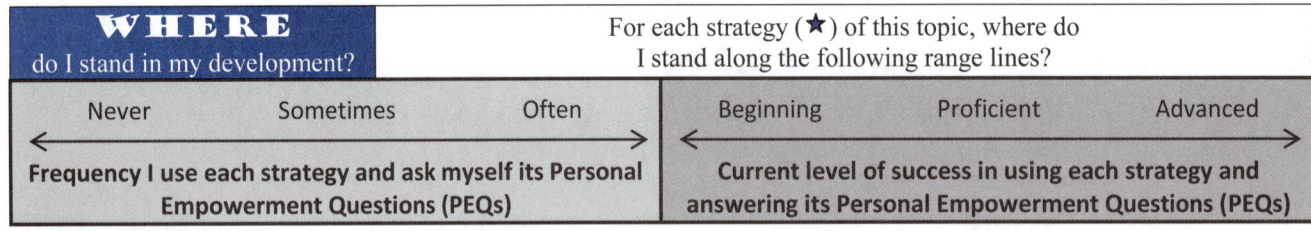

WHERE do I stand in my development?	For each strategy (★) of this topic, where do I stand along the following range lines?	
Never Sometimes Often	Beginning Proficient Advanced	
Frequency I use each strategy and ask myself its Personal Empowerment Questions (PEQs)	Current level of success in using each strategy and answering its Personal Empowerment Questions (PEQs)	

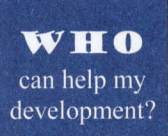 **WHO** can help my development?

- In addition to using the range lines above for self-assessment, I can ask others (parents, teachers, mentors, and peers) to assess me so that I can learn and grow from their observations and input.
- I can observe the ways in which other people approach the skills I want to learn. What do other people do well? What do they need to improve? How can I use their example to improve myself?
- I can talk to other people about how they approach the skills I want to develop. I can ask what strategies they use to be successful.

Being Creative

Understanding and Interacting with Others
1. Understanding What Makes People Tick
(Recognizing the Wants, Needs, and Motivations of Others)

WHY do I need this skill?	By understanding what makes people "tick" (their wants, needs, and motivations), I can help a customer better understand a product, meet the needs of a client, work with my teammates at my job, motivate others, lead a group, interpret others' ideas, empathize, predict what people will want from me, and better communicate in my personal life. *I should strive to understand what makes others "tick" so that I can maximize my potential in a variety of social interactions.*
HOW will I develop this skill?	I will *ask* myself the ❓ Personal Empowerment Questions (PEQs) and strive to *affirm* the • Personal Empowerment Statements (PESs) below.

★ In school, the workplace, and everyday life, I will strive to understand what makes people tick.
❓ I will ask Personal Empowerment Questions (PEQs) like those below.
• I will strive to affirm Personal Empowerment Statements (PESs) like those below.

UNDERSTANDING WHAT MAKES PEOPLE TICK
(RECOGNIZING THE WANTS, NEEDS, AND MOTIVATIONS OF OTHERS)

❓ What does that person need or want?
❓ What want or need led that person to do ____?
❓ Why is that ____ important to them?
❓ What makes them happy or unhappy?
❓ What do I need or want?
❓ Why do I do certain things or see things in a certain way?
❓ Why is that ____ important to me?
❓ What makes me happy or unhappy?
❓ Why might that person have a differing view?
❓ Where is our common ground?
❓ How can I use my understanding of others to improve communication, collaboration, motivation, and leadership?

❓ How can I add a personal touch to my interactions with others in order to appeal to their wants, needs, and motivations?

• I am developing a better understanding of my own and other peoples' wants, needs, motivations, and values.
• By better understanding what makes people tick, I have better interactions with others.

WHERE do I stand in my development?	For this topic, where do I stand along the following range lines?
Never Sometimes Often ⟵————————————⟶ Frequency that I seek to understand what makes people tick, ask myself the Personal Empowerment Questions (PEQs), and affirm the Personal Empowerment Statements (PESs)	Beginning Proficient Advanced ⟵————————————⟶ Current level of skill in understanding what makes people tick, answering the Personal Empowerment Questions (PEQs), and affirming the Personal Empowerment Statements (PESs)

 **WHO** can help my development?	• In addition to using the range lines above for self-assessment, I can ask others (parents, teachers, mentors, and peers) to assess me so that I can learn and grow from their observations and input. • I can observe the ways in which other people approach the skills I want to learn. What do other people do well? What do they need to improve? How can I use their example to improve myself? • I can talk to other people about how they approach the skills I want to develop. I can ask what strategies they use to be successful.

Understanding and Interacting with Others
2. Using Effective Communication and Social Skills

WHY do I need this skill?	The ability to use effective communication and social skills is critical for interacting with people in the work world and in personal life. *I should develop effective communication and social skills so that I can have successful and meaningful interactions with others.*
HOW will I develop this skill?	Below, there are some strategies (★) for effective communication and social skills. To help myself use these strategies, I will *ask* myself the ❓ Personal Empowerment Questions (PEQs) and strive to *affirm* the • Personal Empowerment Statements (PESs).

★ **In school, the workplace, and everyday life, I will use the strategies below.**
❓ **I will ask Personal Empowerment Questions (PEQs) like those below.**
• **I will strive to affirm Personal Empowerment Statements (PESs) like those below.**

 ## USING EFFECTIVE COMMUNICATION AND SOCIAL SKILLS

 ### USING EFFECTIVE SPEAKING SKILLS

❓ What is my goal in speaking?
❓ What are the expectations of my audience?
❓ What do I need to say to make my point?
❓ How can I engage and connect with my audience?

❓ Am I audible and articulate?
❓ What is my body language saying?

• With thoughtful words and an appropriate demeanor, I can engage my audience.

 ### ASSESSING HOW OTHERS PERCEIVE AND INTERPRET ME

❓ Based on the reactions of my audience, am I being understood?
❓ Am I being interpreted in the manner in which I intend?
❓ What misconceptions might my audience have?
❓ How do my actions and speech make others feel?

❓ Do you (audience member) have any questions or is there something that I can clarify?

• By carefully assessing my audience, I can determine how well I am understood and what steps to take to improve the audience's experience.

USING EFFECTIVE LISTENING SKILLS

❓ Do I look engaged and interested?
❓ Are my actions putting the speaker at ease?
❓ Am I using proper eye contact, body language, posture, questions, and responses?
❓ What idea is this person trying to express?

❓ What do I need clarified?

• I strive to understand and show interest in the things other people say.

33

INTERPRETING NONVERBAL COMMUNICATION

- ❓ What does that person's body language suggest about their feelings or intentions?
- ❓ What patterns of behavior do I observe from that person?
- ❓ Is that the normal body language of this person?
- ❓ What cues allow me to know when a person is being sarcastic or using humor?

- • By observing nonverbal cues, I can develop a deeper understanding of others when communicating.

 ## BUILDING POSITIVE INTERACTIONS AND RELATIONSHIPS

- ❓ What impression of myself am I creating?
- ❓ What is appropriate behavior for this situation?
- ❓ Am I exhibiting tact, integrity, respect, courtesy, humility, and a real sense of who I am?
- ❓ Am I being consistent, honest, loyal, and dedicated?
- ❓ Am I following through with my commitments and promises?
- ❓ What can I say or do to make this interaction run smoothly?
- ❓ How should I behave when things don't go well?

- ❓ What communication challenges might I encounter, and how can I proactively diminish potential conflict?
- ❓ How can I positively overcome any differences in opinion?
- ❓ How should people generally treat each other in a positive society, and am I treating others this way?

- • With thoughtful and positive behaviors, I build meaningful interactions and relationships.

 ## PROMOTING MYSELF AND INTERVIEWING

- ❓ In an interview, how should I dress, carry myself, and communicate in order to make a great impression?
- ❓ How can I enhance my networking skills by building positive relationships?
- ❓ How do my social behaviors and communication skills affect my ability to promote myself in the workplace?

- ❓ What are the social expectations in an interview or workplace social interaction?

- • I show my strengths and qualities and appropriately present myself in order to make a great impression and positively promote myself.

WHERE do I stand in my development?	For each strategy (★) of this topic, where do I stand along the following range lines?	
Never　　　Sometimes　　　Often	Beginning　　　Proficient　　　Advanced	
Frequency I use each strategy, ask myself its Personal Empowerment Questions (PEQs), and affirm its Personal Empowerment Statements (PESs)	Current level of success in using each strategy, answering its Personal Empowerment Questions (PEQs), and affirming its Personal Empowerment Statements (PESs)	

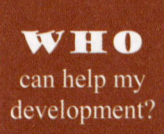

WHO can help my development?	• In addition to using the range lines above for self-assessment, I can ask others (parents, teachers, mentors, and peers) to assess me so that I can learn and grow from their observations and input. • I can observe the ways in which other people approach the skills I want to learn. What do other people do well? What do they need to improve? How can I use their example to improve myself? • I can talk to other people about how they approach the skills I want to develop. I can ask what strategies they use to be successful.

3. Explaining and Presenting Ideas

WHY do I need this skill?	Effective workers can successfully explain and present ideas and information. Plumbers describe plumbing needs to customers, medical doctors clarify diagnoses or procedures to patients and coworkers, and business people give customers details about how products or services work and why those customers need the products or services. *I should develop effective explaining skills so that I can successfully communicate information and ideas in professional and personal life.*
HOW will I develop this skill?	Below, there are some strategies (★) for explaining and presenting ideas. To help myself use these strategies, I will *ask* myself the ❓ Personal Empowerment Questions (PEQs) and strive to *affirm* the • Personal Empowerment Statements (PESs).

★ **In school, the workplace, and everyday life, I will use the strategies below.**
❓ **I will ask Personal Empowerment Questions (PEQs) like those below.**
• **I will strive to affirm Personal Empowerment Statements (PESs) like those below.**

EXPLAINING AND PRESENTING IDEAS

DETERMINING THE GOALS OF MY EXPLANATION

❓ What do I want my listener(s) to get out of this explanation?

❓ Which key ideas will I need to convey in my explanation?

• I know what I want others to understand.

CREATING AN UNDERSTANDABLE SEQUENCE AND FLOW OF INFORMATION

❓ What does the listener need to know first, and how can I build his or her understanding from this starting point?

❓ In what order should I make my points so that I maximize understanding?

❓ What transitions will make my explanation flow well?

• My speaking sequence and flow allow people to easily understand me.

PREDICTING COMMUNICATION CHALLENGES AND POTENTIAL AUDIENCE MISCONCEPTIONS

❓ What are the most difficult aspects of this topic to understand?

❓ What challenges did I encounter when I tried to explain this before?

❓ What did I have trouble understanding when I first learned about this topic?

❓ What can I say or do to avoid these potential challenges?

• I make it easier to understand my explanations by predicting those things that could be misunderstood and working to avoid these misconceptions.

ASSESSING THE PRIOR KNOWLEDGE OF MY AUDIENCE

❓ What does the audience already know?

❓ Considering what the audience already knows, do I need to add or subtract any information from my explanation?

• By determining what the audience already knows, I can make my explanations better suit their needs.

Explaining and Presenting Ideas

CAPTURING ATTENTION, ENGAGING, AND INSPIRING AUDIENCE CONFIDENCE IN ME

- ❓ How can I engage my audience?
- ❓ Why might my listener(s) care about or be excited about the topic that I am explaining and how can I tap into this?
- ❓ How can I convey the real-world value of my topic?
- ❓ What techniques for engagement are appropriate for this setting?
- ❓ How should I carry myself and speak so that I inspire confidence and portray myself as knowledgeable?

- ❓ Am I making eye contact with a variety of people?
- ❓ Will the use of appropriate and non-repetitive gestures help capture attention?
- ❓ What does my body language convey to my audience about my energy and passion for this topic?

- • My energy, passion, and engaging approach draw people into listening to my words.

EXPLAINING WITH CLARITY, CONCISENESS, AND FOCUS

- ❓ Am I speaking clearly / enunciating?
- ❓ Is my speaking volume appropriate for clear communication?
- ❓ Am I moving at a reasonable pace through my explanation?
- ❓ Am I avoiding the use of fillers (such as "um," "like," or "uh") that are distracting?

- ❓ Do I stay focused as I speak so that I do not drift off-topic?
- ❓ What type of language and slang is appropriate for this audience?

- • My use of language is soothing and easy to understand.

USING AIDS FOR UNDERSTANDING

- ❓ Would this be easier to understand with a visual, auditory, or tactile aid for understanding?
- ❓ What aids are available to me and in what ways could I make use of them?
- ❓ What aids would make this more interesting?

- ❓ What aids will actually help me achieve the goals of my explanation, rather than confuse my listeners?

- • When helpful, I use props to grab attention and make myself easier to understand.

ASSESSING AUDIENCE UNDERSTANDING

- ❓ Do you have any questions for me?
- ❓ What can I clarify for you?
- ❓ Can you summarize what I said so far? (This question is good for student explainers to ask during a classroom activity, but not for adults to ask customers, clients, or patients.)

- ❓ Do the facial expressions and body language of my audience suggest that they understand me?

- • I monitor how well people understand me in order to improve further discussion.

SHIFTING EXPLANATION STRATEGIES

- ❓ Is this explanation really working as planned, or should I shift my strategy?
- ❓ Which part of this is the listener not understanding?
- ❓ Is there an example that I can give to clarify what I am saying?
- ❓ Should I try to explain these ideas again in a different order?

- ❓ In what other creative way can I present this information to my audience?

- • I am flexible and shift the way I am explaining when it is clear that my first approach is not working.

PROMOTING INFORMATION RETENTION
AND REINFORCEMENT IN THE AUDIENCE

❓ How can I draw connections between this information and something else that the audience already understands?

❓ What can I do to help the listener(s) remember the things that I explain?

❓ What are the key ideas of my explanation and how can I summarize them?

• By reviewing and wrapping up what I say, my audience remembers the objectives of my speech.

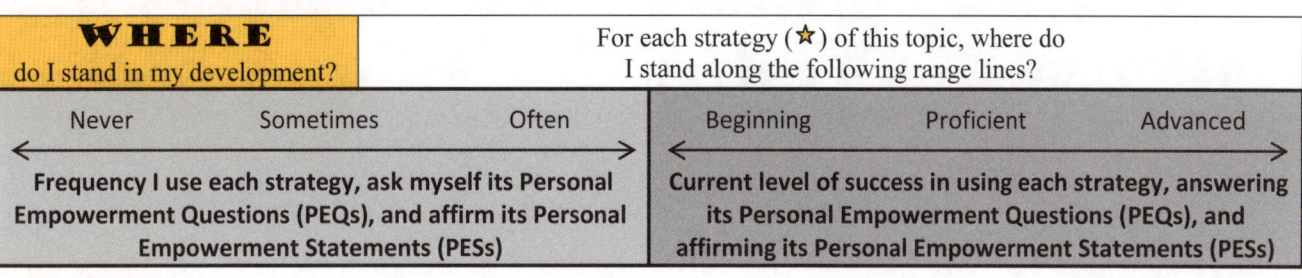

WHERE do I stand in my development?	For each strategy (⭐) of this topic, where do I stand along the following range lines?	
Never Sometimes Often	Beginning Proficient Advanced	
Frequency I use each strategy, ask myself its Personal Empowerment Questions (PEQs), and affirm its Personal Empowerment Statements (PESs)	Current level of success in using each strategy, answering its Personal Empowerment Questions (PEQs), and affirming its Personal Empowerment Statements (PESs)	

WHO can help my development?	• In addition to using the range lines above for self-assessment, I can ask others (parents, teachers, mentors, and peers) to assess me so that I can learn and grow from their observations and input. • I can observe the ways in which other people approach the skills I want to learn. What do other people do well? What do they need to improve? How can I use their example to improve myself? • I can talk to other people about how they approach the skills I want to develop. I can ask what strategies they use to be successful.

Explaining and Presenting Ideas

37

Understanding and Interacting with Others

4. Collaborating through Teamwork

WHY do I need this skill?	In my life, I will be a member of a number of teams in my school, future job, family, community, etc. In all of these teams, we will be working together toward a common goal. *I should develop collaborative teamwork skills so that I can be a positive, supportive, and effective member of my teams.*
HOW will I develop this skill?	Below, there are some strategies (☆) for collaborating through teamwork. To help myself use these strategies, I will *ask* myself the ❓ Personal Empowerment Questions (PEQs) and strive to *affirm* the • Personal Empowerment Statements (PESs).

☆ **In school, the workplace, and everyday life, I will use the strategies below.**
❓ **I will ask Personal Empowerment Questions (PEQs) like those below.**
• **I will strive to affirm Personal Empowerment Statements (PESs) like those below.**

 ## COLLABORATING THROUGH TEAMWORK

 ### CREATING A TEAM ATTITUDE
(WITH RESPECT FOR AND DEDICATION TO THE TEAM)

❓ What is important to my teammates?
❓ Am I contributing to and supporting a positive team attitude?
❓ In what ways do I demonstrate that I am dedicated to and loyal to the team?

❓ In what ways do I demonstrate that I am a happy team player?

• My presence improves the team atmosphere.
• I love being on the team and my teammates can see that.

 ### USING POSITIVE COMMUNICATION

❓ Am I effectively expressing myself to my team?
❓ Am I communicating politely and tactfully?
❓ Am I carefully listening to my teammates and showing interest?

❓ Do I understand or have questions for my teammates?

• I add to the positive communication of this team.

 ### DEMONSTRATING MUTUAL RESPONSIBILITY AND SUPPORT

❓ How do I support the success of my teammates?
❓ What are my responsibilities as a team member?
❓ Am I doing my share of the team's work?
❓ What more can I do to help the team succeed?
❓ In what role can I best support the success of the team?

• We work as a team and succeed as a team.
• If we don't meet our goals, we figure out how to find success ... together.
• We are responsible to the team.

 ### BUILDING UPON AND RESPECTING EACH OTHER'S IDEAS

❓ How can I encourage my teammates to share their ideas?
❓ How can I add to or tweak my teammates' ideas?
❓ How can I be tactful in giving feedback on my teammates' ideas?
❓ What ideas can I offer the team?

❓ What idea(s) will give our team the best chance of success?

• We respectfully work together to develop our best ideas.

MOTIVATING EACH OTHER

- ❓ How can I show my own excitement?
- ❓ What makes my teammates tick? (What are their wants, needs, and desires?)
- ❓ What actions and words can I use to motivate my teammates?
- ❓ What roles would bring out the best in each of our team members?

- ❓ How can I "spice up" the work environment to make team members have more fun?

- • We bring out the best in each other.

 ## RELYING ON EACH OTHER BEFORE SEEKING OUTSIDE HELP

- ❓ What skills, tools, and resources can we use or access in order to accomplish this task on our own?
- ❓ Now that we have made every effort to be independent, with what tasks or tools do we need help?

- • I trust my teammates.
- • We can do this!

 ## FINDING COMMON GROUND

- ❓ What are our goals?
- ❓ What suggestions are my teammates offering?
- ❓ What are my ideas for the team?
- ❓ Which ideas will work the best for our team's goals?
- ❓ What criteria can we use to make tough choices as a team?

- ❓ Can we integrate each other's ideas together?

- • We don't always agree, but we seek and find a shared vision for our team that will lead to success.

Collaborating through Teamwork

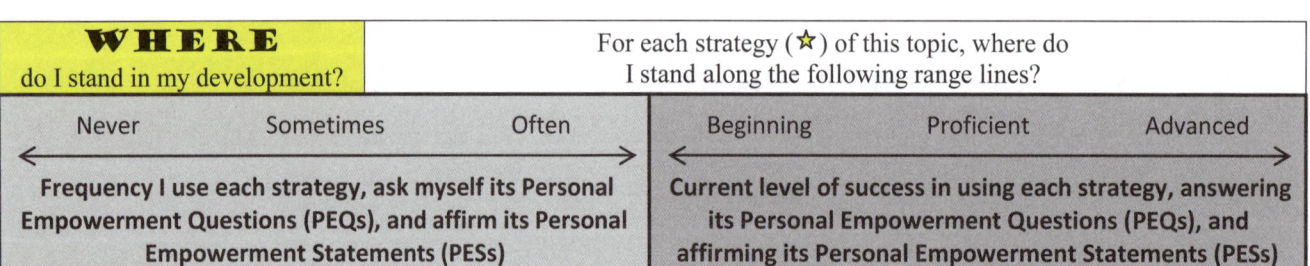

WHERE do I stand in my development?	For each strategy (⭐) of this topic, where do I stand along the following range lines?	
Never　　　Sometimes　　　Often ⟵————————————⟶ Frequency I use each strategy, ask myself its Personal Empowerment Questions (PEQs), and affirm its Personal Empowerment Statements (PESs)	Beginning　　　Proficient　　　Advanced ⟵————————————⟶ Current level of success in using each strategy, answering its Personal Empowerment Questions (PEQs), and affirming its Personal Empowerment Statements (PESs)	

WHO can help my development?	• In addition to using the range lines above for self-assessment, I can ask others (parents, teachers, mentors, and peers) to assess me so that I can learn and grow from their observations and input. • I can observe the ways in which other people approach the skills I want to learn. What do other people do well? What do they need to improve? How can I use their example to improve myself? • I can talk to other people about how they approach the skills I want to develop. I can ask what strategies they use to be successful.

40

5. Competing

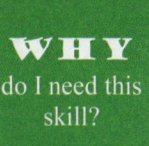 **WHY** do I need this skill?	The world is filled with competitive situations. Potential employees compete for jobs, businesses for customers, lawyers for clients, workers for promotions, teenagers for admission into colleges, politicians for votes, etc. In a global and technological economy, we compete with foreign workers and automated machines for jobs. Life presents us with many opportunities to succeed in competition and get what we want … or not. *I should learn skills that will help me and my teams succeed in competitive situations. Also, I should learn how to use both successes and disappointments in competition as opportunities to learn and grow.*
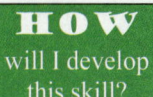 **HOW** will I develop this skill?	Below, there are some strategies (★) for succeeding in and learning from competitive situations. To help myself use these strategies, I will *ask* myself the ❓ Personal Empowerment Questions (PEQs) and strive to *affirm* the • Personal Empowerment Statements (PESs).

★ **In school, the workplace, and everyday life, I will use the strategies below.**
❓ **I will ask Personal Empowerment Questions (PEQs) like those below.**
• **I will strive to affirm Personal Empowerment Statements (PESs) like those below.**

 **COMPETING**

Knowing How to Prepare for and Succeed in Competitive Situations

 HAVING A PROPER WORK ETHIC IN PREPARATION FOR COMPETITION

❓ What are my (our) goals and dreams in this competition?
❓ How will I (we) succeed in this competition?
❓ Why should I (we) be confident in this competition?
❓ What might I (we) have to sacrifice in order to win?
❓ What obstacles will I (we) have to overcome to win?

❓ In what ways am I responsible for my own and my teammates' successes?

• I know my competitive goals and am prepared to succeed.

 CONSIDERING THE COMPETITORS

❓ What are my (our) competitors doing or planning to do in order to win?
❓ How will I (we) prepare for and react to the competition's actions?
❓ What preparations, skills, or plans will most likely help us beat another team?

❓ What might my (our) competitors do to satisfy the needs and wants of customers, clients, or patients, and what do I (we) need to do to better satisfy them? (PEQ for adults)

• I (We) understand my (our) competitors and will meet the challenges they pose.

HAVING A PROPER STATE OF MIND IN COMPETITION

- ❓ Where should my (our) focus lie in order to be successful?
- ❓ What is a positive, appropriate, and determined way for me (us) to react when competitors do well or get an edge?
- ❓ When is it in my (our) best interest to focus more on my (our) own actions, rather than on the competitor's actions?

- • I (we) can do this!
- • I am (we are) looking forward to the challenge.
- • I (we) can overcome any obstacles.

DISPLAYING PROPER DEMEANOR
(SPORTSMANSHIP)

- ❓ How does my (our) behavior affect the integrity of this competition or situation?
- ❓ How should I (we) behave in order to show respect, humility, maturity, and integrity?

- ❓ What will be the consequences of immature behavior on my (our) part?

- • I am a good sport who shows integrity, respect, humility, and maturity.

Learning from Wins and Losses after a Competition

ASSESSING AND LEARNING FROM MY PERFORMANCE AND MY TEAM'S PERFORMANCE

- ❓ Which strategies worked well and which did not?
- ❓ In which areas was I (were we) well prepared and not well prepared?
- ❓ What should I (we) do the same and what should I (we) do differently in the next competition?

- ❓ Which team roles did and did not work?

- • Based on my (our) performance, I (we) know what can be done to improve future performances.

ASSESSING AND LEARNING FROM THE PERFORMANCE OF MY COMPETITORS

- ❓ What did my (our) competitors do well and what did they not do well?
- ❓ What can I (we) learn from my (our) competitors to help me (us) improve?
- ❓ What did my (our) competitors probably learn from my (our) performance and their own performance?

- ❓ In what ways will my (our) competitors probably react and change in light of this competition?

- • Based my (our) competitors' performance, I (we) know what can be done to improve future success.

LEARNING THE "INS" AND "OUTS" OF THE COMPETITION

- ❓ What are the rules, common practices, etiquette, and environmental factors associated with this type of competition?
- ❓ In previous competitions, what was and what was not in my (our) control?
- ❓ In previous competitions, what happened that I (we) did not expect, but should expect in the future?

- ❓ Considering the rules, common practices, etiquette, and environmental factors associated with this type of activity, which strategies will allow me (us) to maximize my (our) performance in the future?

- • I am (We are) developing a better understanding of the "ins" and "outs" of this competition, and it will help in the future.

Competing

DEVELOPING NEW STRATEGIES OVER TIME

- ❔ What is working well in my (our) competitive endeavors?
- ❔ What competitive strategies need to change?
- ❔ What new strategies are necessary for continued success in competitive situations?

- • I am (We are) finding new ways to be successful in competition.

 ## FINDING POSITIVES IN AND MOTIVATION FROM COMPETITION

- ❔ What did I (we) do well in this competition?
- ❔ How can I (we) turn this success into more successes and more motivation?
- ❔ How can I (we) use this disappointment for motivation?

- ❔ Why should I (we) be proud?

- • My (Our) experiences are giving me (us) motivation for future competition.

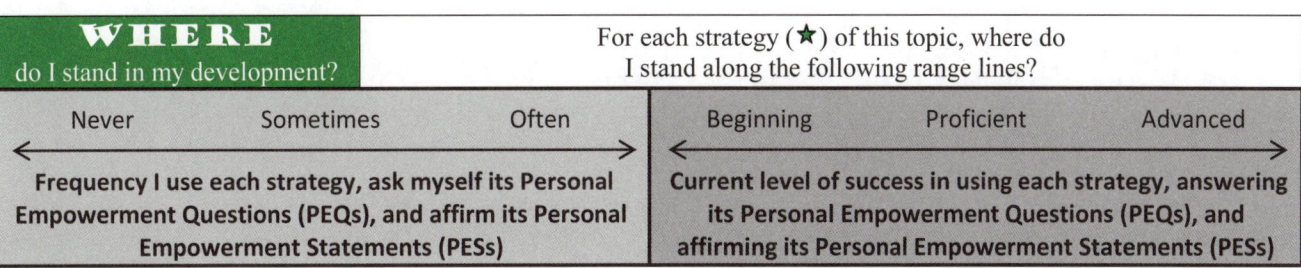

WHERE do I stand in my development?	For each strategy (★) of this topic, where do I stand along the following range lines?	
Never Sometimes Often ⟵──────────────⟶ **Frequency I use each strategy, ask myself its Personal Empowerment Questions (PEQs), and affirm its Personal Empowerment Statements (PESs)**	Beginning Proficient Advanced ⟵──────────────⟶ **Current level of success in using each strategy, answering its Personal Empowerment Questions (PEQs), and affirming its Personal Empowerment Statements (PESs)**	

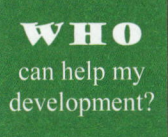

WHO can help my development?	• In addition to using the range lines above for self-assessment, I can ask others (parents, teachers, mentors, and peers) to assess me so that I can learn and grow from their observations and input. • I can observe the ways in which other people approach the skills I want to learn. What do other people do well? What do they need to improve? How can I use their example to improve myself? • I can talk to other people about how they approach the skills I want to develop. I can ask what strategies they use to be successful.

Personal Skills, Attitudes, and Habits
1. Setting Goals

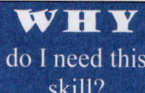 **WHY** do I need this skill?

To find success in my life, I will need goals. Goals will provide the motivation and vision for me to create a pathway to success and diligently follow it. *I should develop the ability to set and work toward goals that will bring me personal and professional success and satisfaction.*

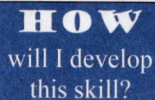 **HOW** will I develop this skill?

Below, there are some strategies (★) for setting and working toward goals. To help myself use these strategies, I will *ask* myself the ❓ Personal Empowerment Questions (PEQs) and strive to *affirm* the • Personal Empowerment Statements (PESs).

★ **In school, the workplace, and everyday life, I will use the strategies below.**
❓ **I will ask Personal Empowerment Questions (PEQs) like those below.**
• **I will strive to affirm Personal Empowerment Statements (PESs) like those below.**

 ## SETTING GOALS

 ### DEVELOPING A VISION AND DREAMING

❓ What is my vision or dream?
❓ Why is this vision or dream important to me?
❓ What do I have to gain?
❓ What will my future look like when I succeed?
❓ Why should I be intrinsically motivated to work hard?

❓ I want to be realistic, but am I selling myself short ... I know that I can accomplish great things!

• I can see myself achieving my vision and dreams.

DEVELOPING SHORT-TERM AND LONG-TERM GOALS
(PATHWAY TO SUCCESS)

❓ What do I need to accomplish to meet my dreams and vision?
❓ What short-term and long-term goals will lead me to ultimate success?
❓ What steps do I need to take to achieve these goals?
❓ How can I compartmentalize the steps of this task in order to make it feel less overwhelming?

❓ How will I know if my goals are being met ... how will I measure success?
❓ What resources can I use to accomplish my goals?
❓ How do others accomplish similar goals?

• By working toward the short-term and long-term goals I have created, I will achieve my dreams.

 ### ASSESSING PROGRESS AND MODIFYING PATHWAYS AS NEEDED

❓ How am I progressing toward my short-term and long-term goals?
❓ In which successes can I take pride?
❓ In what ways do I need to improve my actions in order to better achieve my goals?

❓ Are my short-term goals helping me achieve my long-term goals? If not, what modifications should I make?

• I am monitoring my progress and actively working to meet my goals.

Setting Goals

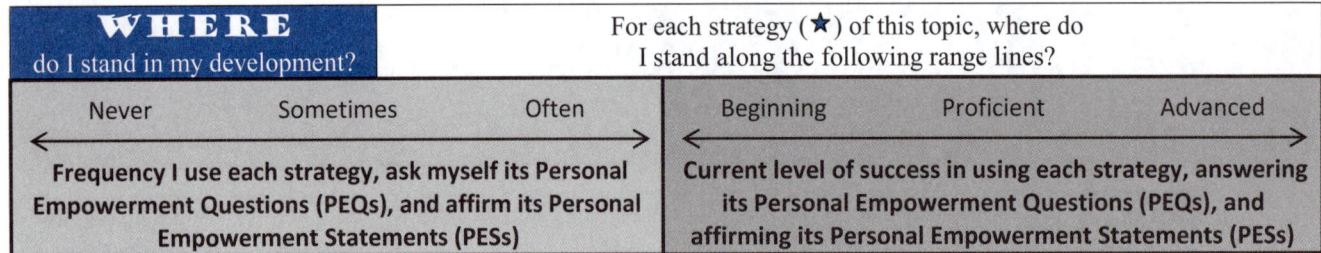

WHERE do I stand in my development?	For each strategy (★) of this topic, where do I stand along the following range lines?	
Never Sometimes Often ⟵————————————⟶ **Frequency I use each strategy, ask myself its Personal Empowerment Questions (PEQs), and affirm its Personal Empowerment Statements (PESs)**	Beginning Proficient Advanced ⟵————————————⟶ **Current level of success in using each strategy, answering its Personal Empowerment Questions (PEQs), and affirming its Personal Empowerment Statements (PESs)**	

WHO can help my development?	• In addition to using the range lines above for self-assessment, I can ask others (parents, teachers, mentors, and peers) to assess me so that I can learn and grow from their observations and input. • I can observe the ways in which other people approach the skills I want to learn. What do other people do well? What do they need to improve? How can I use their example to improve myself? • I can talk to other people about how they approach the skills I want to develop. I can ask what strategies they use to be successful.

Setting Goals

Personal Skills, Attitudes, and Habits
2. Employing a Proper Work Ethic

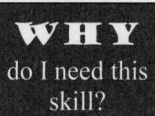 **WHY** do I need this skill?	The biggest factor in my life's successes will be my devotion to responsibly working hard for what I want. *I should develop a great work ethic so that I carry a positive attitude as I proactively and persistently work to overcome challenges, overcome setbacks, and achieve my goals.*
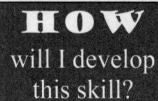 **HOW** will I develop this skill?	Below, there are some strategies (★) for employing a proper work ethic. To help myself use these strategies, I will *ask* myself the ❓ Personal Empowerment Questions (PEQs) and strive to *affirm* the • Personal Empowerment Statements (PESs).

★ **In school, the workplace, and everyday life, I will use the strategies below.**
❓ **I will ask Personal Empowerment Questions (PEQs) like those below.**
• **I will strive to affirm Personal Empowerment Statements (PESs) like those below.**

 ## EMPLOYING A PROPER WORK ETHIC

 ### HAVING AN EMPOWERING AND POSITIVE ATTITUDE

- ❓ What skills and habits do I have that will allow me to succeed?
- ❓ What empowering resources can I use to accomplish my goals?
- ❓ Who can help me achieve my goals?
- ❓ What things did I do when I experienced success in the past?
- ❓ In what ways am I in control of the outcome of my journey to succeed?

- ❓ How can I have fun while working toward my goals?

- • I am prepared and capable … I can do this!
- • If I don't already know how to do something, I can learn how.
- • I am proud of my successes.

 ### SACRIFICING

- ❓ What sacrifices might be necessary to achieve my vision?
- ❓ When might sacrifices need to be made?
- ❓ How will my sacrifices help me achieve my goals?

- ❓ Why are the sacrifices worth it?
- ❓ How will I persuade myself to make sacrifices?

- • I make sacrifices that will pay off in the future.

STAYING THE COURSE / PERSISTING

- ❓ What dreams and goals do I want to achieve?
- ❓ How will I know if I have encountered an obstacle or I am off course?
- ❓ What obstacles can I expect to encounter?
- ❓ What will I do if I get sidetracked from achieving my goals by predictable or unpredictable obstacles?
- ❓ What do I stand to lose if I don't stay the course?

- ❓ Who is counting on me to succeed?
- ❓ Who or what can help me stay on course to achieve my goals?
- ❓ How is this obstacle an opportunity?

- • I will fight through challenges and achieve my goals.
- • I will stay the course.

ACTING PROACTIVELY

- ❓ What might I have to overcome to achieve my goals?
- ❓ How might I get sidetracked?
- ❓ What will I likely need in the future to accomplish my goals?
- ❓ What can I do now that will make me more prepared later?

- ❓ What support structure can I put in place to deal with unexpected problems?

- • I am readying myself for the challenges I will or might face.

BEHAVING WITH PERSONAL RESPONSIBILITY / ACCOUNTABILITY

- ❓ What are the consequences of my actions or inaction?
- ❓ In what ways am I in control of my own destiny?
- ❓ Why is my own hard work the most important factor in my success?

- ❓ What are my responsibilities?

- • I am responsible for my success.
- • The actions I take have consequences. I plan to create positive consequences.

TAKING INITIATIVE WITH SELF-DIRECTION AND INDEPENDENCE

- ❓ Without waiting for someone to tell me what I should do, what goals can I set out to accomplish?
- ❓ What plans can I create for myself?
- ❓ How can I take control of my own success?

- ❓ How can I become more independent?
- ❓ Why is it crucial for my long-term success that I behave in a self-directed manner?

- • I can direct myself to succeed.

SHOWING RESPONSIBILITY TO OTHERS
(FAMILY, TEAM, SCHOOL, COMMUNITY, AND COUNTRY)

- ❓ What is my role in this group, and what do I need to do to meet my responsibilities?
- ❓ Why does my participation and hard work matter to the group?
- ❓ What do we have at stake?
- ❓ How can I use what I'm learning in class to benefit my family, team, school, community, or country?

- ❓ How can I demonstrate respect for others?
- ❓ How can I be charitable and helpful?
- ❓ Who is counting on me in this family, team, school, community, or country?

- • My team needs me, and I will do my part to help us succeed.

GIVING QUALITY PERFORMANCE ... NOT JUST BEING PRESENT

- ❓ Is this the best that I can do?
- ❓ In what ways can I maximize my potential?
- ❓ In what ways is simply being present not good enough for success?

- • It's not good enough to just show up. I will work to meet my potential.

WHERE do I stand in my development?	For each strategy (★) of this topic, where do I stand along the following range lines?	
Never Sometimes Often	Beginning Proficient Advanced	
Frequency I use each strategy, ask myself its Personal Empowerment Questions (PEQs), and affirm its Personal Empowerment Statements (PESs)	Current level of success in using each strategy, answering its Personal Empowerment Questions (PEQs), and affirming its Personal Empowerment Statements (PESs)	

|  **WHO** can help my development? | • In addition to using the range lines above for self-assessment, I can ask others (parents, teachers, mentors, and peers) to assess me so that I can learn and grow from their observations and input.
• I can observe the ways in which other people approach the skills I want to learn. What do other people do well? What do they need to improve? How can I use their example to improve myself?
• I can talk to other people about how they approach the skills I want to develop. I can ask what strategies they use to be successful. |

Personal Skills, Attitudes, and Habits

3. Adapting, Changing, and Being Versatile

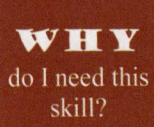

WHY do I need this skill?	In the 21st century, change is constant. There are always new technologies, new types of jobs, new circumstances in the workplace, and new circumstances in society. *Thus, I should be prepared to adapt to a changing world, have a versatile skill set, and have a flexible attitude toward change.* This will allow me to be more valuable in the work world and successful in my endeavors.
HOW will I develop this skill?	Below, there are some strategies (★) for adapting, changing, and being versatile. To help myself use these strategies, I will *ask* myself the ❓ Personal Empowerment Questions (PEQs) and strive to *affirm* the • Personal Empowerment Statements (PESs).

★ **In school, the workplace, and everyday life, I will use the strategies below.**
❓ **I will ask Personal Empowerment Questions (PEQs) like those below.**
• **I will strive to affirm Personal Empowerment Statements (PESs) like those below.**

ADAPTING, CHANGING, AND BEING VERSATILE

IDENTIFYING NEW CIRCUMSTANCES AND EXPECTATIONS

❓ What are the expectations in this new situation or place?
❓ What is my role in this new situation or place?
❓ What do I expect when changes occur (based on my previous experiences with changes)?

• I know what it takes to be successful here.

ACQUIRING THE RESOURCES AND SKILLS NEEDED

❓ What resources and skills do I already have?
❓ What new resources and skills do I need to be successful under these new circumstances?
❓ How and where can I acquire these new resources and skills?

• I have and will acquire those things that I need to be successful.

FINDING COMFORT AND CONFIDENCE IN CHANGE

❓ What might I fear in this change?
❓ What is unfamiliar?
❓ What can I do to overcome any anxiety or unfamiliarity?
❓ How can I get some consistency in my life?
❓ What reasons do I have to be confident during this change?

• I know the potential sources of anxiety and I am addressing them.
• I will make it through this change to a place of higher familiarity, consistency, and peace of mind.

EXPECTING CHANGE

❷ Considering the current trends, what changes are likely to occur?
❷ What changes are not likely, but could happen?
❷ What do I need to do to prepare myself for potential changes?
❷ What new work and technical skills will make me more adaptable, versatile, and prepared for future circumstances?

• I know that change will come, and I am continuously preparing myself.

WHERE do I stand in my development?	For each strategy (★) of this topic, where do I stand along the following range lines?	
Never Sometimes Often ⟵──────────────────────⟶ **Frequency I use each strategy, ask myself its Personal Empowerment Questions (PEQs), and affirm its Personal Empowerment Statements (PESs)**	Beginning Proficient Advanced ⟵──────────────────────⟶ **Current level of success in using each strategy, answering its Personal Empowerment Questions (PEQs), and affirming its Personal Empowerment Statements (PESs)**	

WHO can help my development?	• In addition to using the range lines above for self-assessment, I can ask others (parents, teachers, mentors, and peers) to assess me so that I can learn and grow from their observations and input. • I can observe the ways in which other people approach the skills I want to learn. What do other people do well? What do they need to improve? How can I use their example to improve myself? • I can talk to other people about how they approach the skills I want to develop. I can ask what strategies they use to be successful.

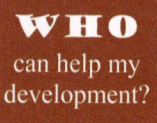

4. Managing Stress

WHY do I need this skill?	In my future, I will encounter a variety of challenges as I navigate my personal life, compete for work, and adapt to a constantly changing world. These challenges will create varying levels of stress throughout life. *I should develop the ability to manage stress so that I can live a more successful and fulfilling life.*
HOW will I develop this skill?	Below, there are some strategies (☆) for managing stress. To help myself use these strategies, I will *ask* myself the ❓ Personal Empowerment Questions (PEQs) and strive to *affirm* the • Personal Empowerment Statements (PESs).

☆ In school, the workplace, and everyday life, I will use the strategies below.
❓ I will ask Personal Empowerment Questions (PEQs) like those below.
• I will strive to affirm Personal Empowerment Statements (PESs) like those below.

 **MANAGING STRESS**

 ADDRESSING THE SOURCE OF MY STRESS

- ❓ What is causing this stress?
- ❓ Can I reduce or eliminate the sources of stress?
- ❓ Can I compartmentalize the sources of stress in order to keep them from affecting other parts of my life?
- ❓ Can I use some stresses to perform better?

- • I am finding ways to reduce sources of negative stress.
- • I am using certain minor stresses to my advantage.

 DIFFUSING MY STRESS

- ❓ What activities make me content and relaxed?
- ❓ What environment and people reduce my stress?
- ❓ What can I do to shift my attention away from this stress?

- • I know how to let things go and find relaxation.

☆ **PICKING MY BATTLES**

- ❓ How important to me is this problem?
- ❓ Is this issue worth worrying about?
- ❓ What is or is not in my control?
- ❓ Is worrying about this issue helping me or changing anything? If not, should I let it go?

- • I know which things are not truly worthy of creating stress. I let them go.

WHERE do I stand in my development?	For each strategy (★) of this topic, where do I stand along the following range lines?	
Never Sometimes Often ⟷	Beginning Proficient Advanced ⟷	
Frequency I use each strategy, ask myself its Personal Empowerment Questions (PEQs), and affirm its Personal Empowerment Statements (PESs)	**Current level of success in using each strategy, answering its Personal Empowerment Questions (PEQs), and affirming its Personal Empowerment Statements (PESs)**	

WHO can help my development?	• In addition to using the range lines above for self-assessment, I can ask others (parents, teachers, mentors, and peers) to assess me so that I can learn and grow from their observations and input. • I can observe the ways in which other people approach the skills I want to learn. What do other people do well? What do they need to improve? How can I use their example to improve myself? • I can talk to other people about how they approach the skills I want to develop. I can ask what strategies they use to be successful.

Managing Stress

Personal Skills, Attitudes, and Habits
5. Being Organized and Efficient

WHY do I need this skill?	For everyone including clerks, doctors, teachers, engineers, hairdressers, business owners, carpenters, parents, and students, being organized and efficient is crucial. These skills allow us to make the best use of our time and resources. *I should develop the ability to be organized and efficient in school, in work, and in my everyday life so that I can achieve my goals.*
HOW will I develop this skill?	Below, there are some strategies (☆) for being organized and efficient. To help myself use these strategies, I will *ask* myself the ❓ Personal Empowerment Questions (PEQs) and strive to *affirm* the • Personal Empowerment Statements (PESs).

☆ In school, the workplace, and everyday life, I will use the strategies below.
❓ I will ask Personal Empowerment Questions (PEQs) like those below.
• I will strive to affirm Personal Empowerment Statements (PESs) like those below.

 **BEING ORGANIZED AND EFFICIENT**

 FOCUSING ON MY GOALS AND MAKING PLANS

- ❓ What do I want to achieve?
- ❓ What actions must I take to achieve my goals?
- ❓ What actions tend to lead me away from following my plans of action and away from achieving my goals? How can I deal with these issues?

- • I make plans and take actions that actually lead to my goals.

 MANAGING MY TIME

- ❓ What tasks do I need to accomplish and when can I do them?
- ❓ What are my priorities?
- ❓ How can I create the necessary time for my tasks?
- ❓ How can I most efficiently use the time available?
- ❓ Should I multitask to get more than one thing done at a time?

- ❓ What tools can I use to help manage my time?
- ❓ How will I know that I am on track to achieve my goals?
- ❓ Considering my current progress, do my plans need to be modified?

- • Due to my organized and efficient use of time, I can accomplish all of my goals.

 MANAGING MY RESOURCES FOR ORGANIZATION AND EFFICIENCY

- ❓ What tasks do I need to accomplish?
- ❓ What resources are available, and what resources will best help me perform my tasks?
- ❓ Who can help me in accomplishing my goals?
- ❓ What will be the most efficient use of my resources?
- ❓ Is there an easier way to do this task?

- ❓ What resources are actually helping, and what resources can I do without?

- • With the proper strategies and tools, I can efficiently manage tasks as I work toward my goals.

| **WHERE** | For each strategy (★) of this topic, where do |
| do I stand in my development? | I stand along the following range lines? |

Never Sometimes Often	Beginning Proficient Advanced
Frequency I use each strategy, ask myself its Personal Empowerment Questions (PEQs), and affirm its Personal Empowerment Statements (PESs)	Current level of success in using each strategy, answering its Personal Empowerment Questions (PEQs), and affirming its Personal Empowerment Statements (PESs)

| **WHO** can help my development? | • In addition to using the range lines above for self-assessment, I can ask others (parents, teachers, mentors, and peers) to assess me so that I can learn and grow from their observations and input.
• I can observe the ways in which other people approach the skills I want to learn. What do other people do well? What do they need to improve? How can I use their example to improve myself?
• I can talk to other people about how they approach the skills I want to develop. I can ask what strategies they use to be successful. |

Being Organized and Efficient

6. Behaving Ethically

WHY do I need this skill?	Our society is best when our citizens act with ethical and principled behaviors that show integrity. *I should strive to act in an ethical manner that will allow me to live a proud, meaningful, and satisfying life in my career and with my family and friends.*
HOW will I develop this skill?	I will *ask* myself the ❓ Personal Empowerment Questions (PEQs) and strive to *affirm* the • Personal Empowerment Statements (PESs) below.

★ In school, the workplace, and everyday life, I will strive to behave ethically.

❓ I will ask Personal Empowerment Questions (PEQs) like those below.

• I will strive to affirm Personal Empowerment Statements (PESs) like those below.

BEHAVING IN AN ETHICAL MANNER THAT SHOWS INTEGRITY

❓ What is ethical behavior?

❓ What are my principles for behavior?

❓ How do my actions affect other people?

❓ Why will cheating hurt me in the long run?

❓ Why would it be unfair to my peers if I were to cheat?

❓ Why is it important to work hard for the things I would like to achieve, rather than taking unethical shortcuts?

• Because of my ethical behavior and integrity, I can be proud of my actions, and I can earn peoples' trust.

WHERE do I stand in my development?	For this topic, where do I stand along the following range lines?

Never Sometimes Often	Beginning Proficient Advanced
← →	← →
Frequency I strive to behave ethically, ask myself the Personal Empowerment Questions (PEQs), and affirm the Personal Empowerment Statements (PESs)	Current level of success in behaving ethically, answering the Personal Empowerment Questions (PEQs), and affirming the Personal Empowerment Statements (PESs)

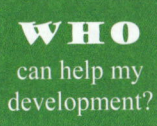

WHO can help my development?	• In addition to using the range lines above for self-assessment, I can ask others (parents, teachers, mentors, and peers) to assess me so that I can learn and grow from their observations and input. • I can observe the ways in which other people approach the skills I want to learn. What do other people do well? What do they need to improve? How can I use their example to improve myself? • I can talk to other people about how they approach the skills I want to develop. I can ask what strategies they use to be successful.

Behaving Ethically

7. Assessing Risks

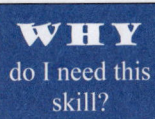 **WHY** do I need this skill?

In my life, there will be various situations in which I will have to weigh the pros and cons of potential decisions in order to assess the risks involved. In these situations, I will need to be able to make challenging decisions with rational thinking. *I should develop the ability to weigh the risks and rewards of my decisions so that I make wise choices in my life.*

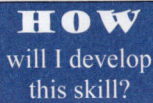 **HOW** will I develop this skill?

I will *ask* myself the ❓ Personal Empowerment Questions (PEQs) and strive to *affirm* the • Personal Empowerment Statements (PESs) below.

★ In school, the workplace, and everyday life, I will assess risks when making complex decisions.
❓ I will ask Personal Empowerment Questions (PEQs) like those below.
• I will strive to affirm Personal Empowerment Statements (PESs) like those below.

ASSESSING RISKS WHEN MAKING COMPLEX DECISIONS

❓ What are the potential positive and negative outcomes that could result from my potential decisions?

❓ What do I want to accomplish, and is it likely that some courses of action are too risky?

❓ Am I thinking carefully about this important decision?

❓ Who might have experiences with this type of choice, and can he or she give me advice?

❓ Am I rushing into this decision, or am I carefully weighing my options?

❓ Who could be affected by my decision?

❓ Considering my goals and the potential consequences of my actions, am I making a responsible decision?

• I carefully and rationally consider the potential risks along with the potential rewards when making complex decisions.

• I make responsible decisions and take responsible risks.

WHERE do I stand in my development?	For this topic, where do I stand along the following range lines?
Never Sometimes Often ⟷	Beginning Proficient Advanced ⟷
Frequency I assess risks, ask myself the Personal Empowerment Questions (PEQs), and affirm the Personal Empowerment Statements (PESs)	Current level of success in assessing risks, answering the Personal Empowerment Questions (PEQs), and affirming the Personal Empowerment Statements (PESs)

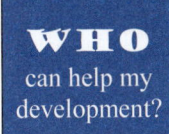 **WHO** can help my development?

• In addition to using the range lines above for self-assessment, I can ask others (parents, teachers, mentors, and peers) to assess me so that I can learn and grow from their observations and input.
• I can observe the ways in which other people approach the skills I want to learn. What do other people do well? What do they need to improve? How can I use their example to improve myself?
• I can talk to other people about how they approach the skills I want to develop. I can ask what strategies they use to be successful.

Assessing Risks

Personal Skills, Attitudes, and Habits
8. Being Financially Literate

WHY do I need this skill?	In life, there are numerous financial decisions that adults must make. Wisely making these choices will allow me to work toward financial stability. *I should develop an understanding of how to make wise financial decisions in my personal and professional life.*
HOW will I develop this skill?	I will *ask* myself the ❓ Personal Empowerment Questions (PEQs) and strive to *affirm* the • Personal Empowerment Statements (PESs) below.

★ **In school, the workplace, and everyday life, I will strive to be financially literate.**
❓ **I will ask Personal Empowerment Questions (PEQs) like those below.**
• **I will strive to affirm Personal Empowerment Statements (PESs) like those below.**

BEING FINANCIALLY LITERATE IN MY PERSONAL AND PROFESSIONAL LIFE

❓ How can I responsibly save or invest my money throughout life?

❓ How can I save for retirement? What are stocks, mutual funds, 401(K)s, IRAs, bonds, and property investments? Which investments and methods of saving money are best for me? How does Social Security work? What is a pension?

❓ How can I avoid unnecessary debt?

❓ What types of insurance are available, and what do I need? What is life insurance? What is disability insurance?

❓ How do I pay my taxes? What are property taxes, and who assesses them? How do I pay federal tax? What is an exemption or a deduction?

❓ How can I start my own business? What licenses are involved? What laws must I consider? How do I go about employing people?

❓ What is a mortgage, and how do I get a mortgage? What is a thirty-year fixed mortgage versus a five-year ARM mortgage?

❓ Should I rent or buy a home?

❓ Should I buy a car, lease a car, or use public transportation?

❓ What are my overall financial goals, and where do I stand in attaining those goals?

❓ What should I be doing right now to achieve my goals for financial security?

• I understand how to manage my financial resources in a responsible manner.

• I know the ways in which I can work toward financial growth and stability.

WHERE do I stand in my development?	For this topic, where do I stand along the following range lines?
Never ⟵ Sometimes Often ⟶	Beginning ⟵ Proficient Advanced ⟶
Frequency I work to develop financial literacy, ask myself the Personal Empowerment Questions (PEQs), and affirm the Personal Empowerment Statements (PESs)	**Current level of success in developing financial literacy, answering the Personal Empowerment Questions (PEQs), and affirming the Personal Empowerment Statements (PESs)**

**WHO** can help my development?	• In addition to using the range lines above for self-assessment, I can ask others (parents, teachers, mentors, and peers) to assess me so that I can learn and grow from their observations and input. • I can observe the ways in which other people approach the skills I want to learn. What do other people do well? What do they need to improve? How can I use their example to improve myself? • I can talk to other people about how they approach the skills I want to develop. I can ask what strategies they use to be successful.

Being Financially
Literate

Using Technology and Media

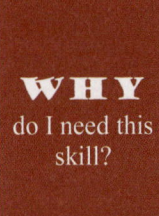

WHY do I need this skill?	New and rapidly changing technological and media tools are deeply interwoven within our workplace and personal lives. For example, customers can use self-checkout machines, professionals can use handheld PCs, travelers can use smart phones to order airline tickets, businesses can use websites to sell products, and students can learn using the Internet. Technology has drastically changed the ways in which we do business, communicate, learn and study, find information, and so much more. *I should learn to effectively, efficiently, and securely use technological and media tools. In addition, I should develop the ability to assess the accuracy of content on the Internet, maintain privacy online, and assess the potential social safety hazards of the Internet.*
HOW will I develop this skill?	Below, there are some strategies (★) for developing the ability to use technology and media. To help myself use these strategies, I will *ask* myself the ❓ Personal Empowerment Questions (PEQs) and strive to *affirm* the • Personal Empowerment Statements (PESs).

★ **In school, the workplace, and everyday life, I will use the strategies below.**
❓ **I will ask Personal Empowerment Questions (PEQs) like those below.**
• **I will strive to affirm Personal Empowerment Statements (PESs) like those below.**

 ## USING TECHNOLOGY AND MEDIA IN THE REAL WORLD

 ### COMMUNICATING AND COLLABORATING

❓ What goals am I trying to accomplish, and what communication and collaboration tools can help me achieve my goals quicker, more efficiently, and with higher quality?

❓ How can tools (email, text messages, blogs, wikis, social networks, or teleconferences) be used to enhance learning (as a student) or enhance products or services (as an adult)?

❓ How would professionals use this technological tool?

❓ Who is my audience in this communication?

❓ What are the social expectations in this situation, and how should I communicate and behave?

❓ What does my style of communication suggest about me?

• I use technology to efficiently and effectively communicate and collaborate.

• I understand and use the proper communication style and etiquette to suit my digital audience.

 ### PRESENTING AND MODELING

❓ What are my goals in this presentation?
❓ Who is my audience?
❓ What key pieces of information do I want to convey?
❓ What technological tool will best accomplish my goals?

❓ How will I grab attention and keep it using technological tools?

• My technological presentations both engage and inform my audience.

 ### BEING ORGANIZED AND EFFICIENT

❓ What information or process do I need to organize?
❓ In what areas can I become more efficient?
❓ What technological tool(s) can help me achieve my organizational and efficiency goals?

❓ How will I stimulate myself to consistently use the technology?

• My use of technology allows me to be more efficient and productive.

RESEARCHING AND LEARNING

- ❓ What technological tool will help me access the correct information and learn what I want or need to know?
- ❓ What shortcuts or tricks can help me more efficiently use this learning tool?

- ❓ What can I learn using this tool?

- • With technology, I am able to unlock the answers to a seemingly infinite number of questions.

PROMOTING MYSELF
(RESUMES, PORTFOLIOS, AND NETWORKING)

- ❓ What technological tools are available for self-promotion?
- ❓ How can I use technological tools to create a great resume, portfolio, website, and/or video in order to impress potential employers?

- ❓ How can I use technological tools to network in order to acquire a job, clients, and customers?

- • Technology empowers me to network and promote myself in many ways.

PROMOTING MY ORGANIZATIONS
(NETWORKING, ADVERTISING, AND SELLING)

- ❓ What technological tools are available for promoting our organization, networking, advertising, or selling our products and services?
- ❓ How can we use these technological tools to acquire and maintain customers, clients, members, or voters?

- • With technology, we can reach a wider audience for our organization.

CONSUMING GOODS AND SERVICES

- ❓ What technological tools can I use to find and purchase the products and services I need or want?
- ❓ How can I evaluate the quality of various products and services that I find?

- ❓ Which technological tools will save me money and time?

- • With technology, I am an empowered consumer.

DESIGNING PROGRAMS, OBJECTS, TOOLS, AND PROCESSES

- ❓ How can I achieve my goals with the design of a program or website?
- ❓ How can I use technology to design objects and processes?

- ❓ How can I use technology to represent (or model) my objects and processes?

- • I can use technology to design.

ASSESSING THE ACCURACY OF INTERNET AND OTHER MEDIA INFORMATION

- ❓ What are the goals of the people who publish this information?
- ❓ Do the authors have a potential bias or agenda?
- ❓ What proof or research is presented?
- ❓ Is there an opinion or a fact being presented?
- ❓ Where can I learn about an opposing opinion?
- ❓ What are some clues that might make me think that this is or is not a reputable web page?
- ❓ What sources can I use to check the accuracy of this information?

- • I know how to assess the accuracy of things I encounter in various forms of media (Internet, news, TV, etc.).

- • I do not simply accept everything I see and hear from various media sources, and I seek the truth.

PRACTICING SAFE AND PRIVATE INTERNET USE

- ❓ Who has access to my personal information, and can I trust them?
- ❓ What signals indicate that I am encountering a scam?
- ❓ How can I identify a "sketchy" website?
- ❓ What technologies are available to aid me in online protection (such as identity theft protection or Internet security software)?

- ❓ What actions should I take when using technology to keep myself safe?
- ❓ What information do I find if I perform an Internet search of my own name?

- I am very careful to keep my identity and privacy safe when using technology.

RECOGNIZING THE FUTURE IMPLICATIONS OF MY INTERNET USAGE

- ❓ How will this action potentially affect me or others in the future?
- ❓ Who might someday use technology to gain access to this information?
- ❓ Will this information help me or harm me?
- ❓ Will this information help others or harm others?

- What I place on the Internet today can affect me and others for many years to come.
- I am very careful to use technological tools in such a way that I leave a trail of information of which I can be proud.

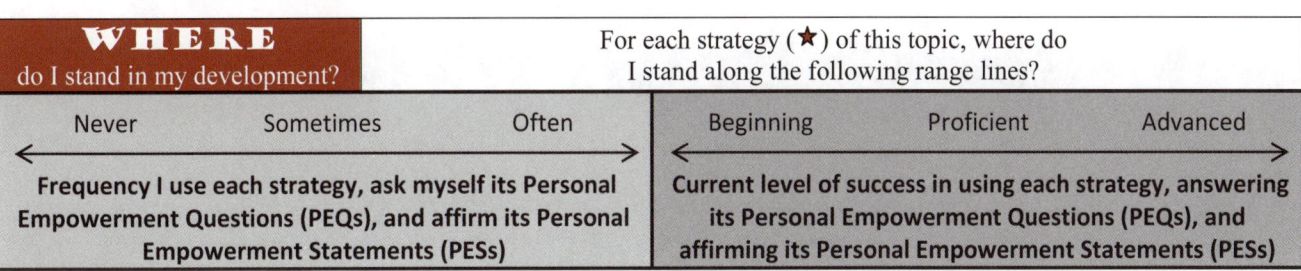

WHERE do I stand in my development?	For each strategy (★) of this topic, where do I stand along the following range lines?
Never Sometimes Often ⟵————————⟶	Beginning Proficient Advanced ⟵————————⟶
Frequency I use each strategy, ask myself its Personal Empowerment Questions (PEQs), and affirm its Personal Empowerment Statements (PESs)	Current level of success in using each strategy, answering its Personal Empowerment Questions (PEQs), and affirming its Personal Empowerment Statements (PESs)

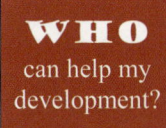

WHO can help my development?

- In addition to using the range lines above for self-assessment, I can ask others (parents, teachers, mentors, and peers) to assess me so that I can learn and grow from their observations and input.
- I can observe the ways in which other people approach the skills I want to learn. What do other people do well? What do they need to improve? How can I use their example to improve myself?
- I can talk to other people about how they approach the skills I want to develop. I can ask what strategies they use to be successful.

Learning Throughout My Life

WHY do I need this skill?	As an adult, I will not always have teachers or mentors to provide me with new information or skills. At times in my work life and personal life, I will need to develop an understanding of new concepts *on my own. I should develop the ability to learn new information and skills and to use my new learning for practical purposes.*
HOW will I develop this skill?	Below, there are some strategies (★) for learning throughout my life. To help myself use these strategies, I will *ask* myself the ❓ Personal Empowerment Questions (PEQs) and strive to *affirm* the • Personal Empowerment Statements (PESs).

★ **In school, the workplace, and everyday life, I will use the strategies below.**
❓ **I will ask Personal Empowerment Questions (PEQs) like those below.**
• **I will strive to affirm Personal Empowerment Statements (PESs) like those below.**

LEARNING BY ASKING CURIOUS QUESTIONS AND SEEKING ANSWERS (INQUIRY)

❓ Why is ____ the way it is?
❓ How does ____ work?
❓ What will happen if ____?
❓ What new questions do I have that I want to answer?
❓ How will I learn the answers to my questions?
❓ How can I (we) figure this out?
❓ How do the discussions, activities, and investigations that we are doing relate to the question(s) I am trying to answer?
❓ How can I use the new pieces of information that I am building to answer the question, understand the process, or understand the phenomenon?

❓ What steps will I need to take to find answers?

• I am curious about the world around me.
• I ask questions and seek answers.
• I piece together the things I learn in discussions, learning activities, and investigations to build understanding.
• I strive to think through and independently discover new learning.
• My teachers are guides in my learning and do not simply "spoon-feed" me information … and this empowers me.

BUILDING ON MY PRIOR KNOWLEDGE

❓ How does this relate to what I already know?
❓ Can I use my prior knowledge to help me understand this new concept?

• I build new understanding by reflecting on and building upon what I already know.

LEARNING LARGER CONCEPTS PIECE BY PIECE

❓ How does this piece of knowledge build on other new concepts that I am learning?
❓ Now that I know this, what else can I learn?
❓ How does this idea fit into the big picture of this topic?

• I construct understanding of larger ideas by building them piece by piece.
• I seek to understand how the smaller pieces of a concept fit together to create the big picture.

USING NEW LEARNING FOR REAL-WORLD TASKS

❓ How can I use this new knowledge or skill to accomplish a task?

❓ In what ways does my new understanding empower me?

• I can perform real-world tasks with the knowledge and skills I learn.

MAKING PERSONAL CONNECTIONS WITH NEW LEARNING

❓ How does this new learning relate to me and the world in which I live?

❓ How does this relate to my future?

❓ How does this affect my opinions?

❓ How does this create challenges?

❓ How can this be used for good?

• The knowledge and skills I learn have everyday relevance to my life.

CREATING DEEP UNDERSTANDING OF NEW CONCEPTS

❓ What is the deeper meaning of this concept?

❓ Why does this process work so well or so poorly?

❓ How did this come to be?

• I work to develop deep understanding when I learn rather than simply scratching the surface.

SUMMARIZING AND SIMPLIFYING NEW CONCEPTS

❓ What are the key words, ideas, and processes that make up this new concept?

❓ How can I make this complex idea simpler?

❓ What are the most important ideas and skills I should get out of learning this concept?

❓ If I had to summarize this new concept or skill in a sentence or two, what would I say?

• When I learn new concepts, I summarize them and look for ways to make complex ideas simpler to understand.

COMPARING AND CONTRASTING NEW CONCEPTS

❓ In what ways is this new concept similar to others?

❓ In what ways is this new concept different from others?

• I can see the ways in which this concept relates to others … I see how it is similar and how it is different.

USING A VARIETY OF METHODS TO LEARN

❓ With which learning tools and strategies do I feel most comfortable?

❓ With which learning tools and strategies do I best understand and retain new concepts?

❓ Different learning strategies and tools seem to be best suited for different learning goals. Which method is best suited for my current learning goal of ____?

• I know which learning tools and strategies work best for me.

• I recognize that learning different types of knowledge and skills might require that I use different types of learning tools and strategies.

Learning Throughout My Life

68

TAKING THE TIME TO FULLY PROCESS NEW IDEAS

- ❓ Stop. Do I understand this?
- ❓ What questions do I have?
- ❓ Am I moving at a reasonable pace for my brain to process this new information?

- • I take time to reflect upon and digest new learning in order to maximize understanding.

BREAKING DOWN NEW TERMS INTO PARTS THAT I UNDERSTAND

- ❓ What similarities does this new word have to those that I already know?
- ❓ Does this term have any root words that give insight into its meaning?
- ❓ What do I predict is the meaning of this word?
- ❓ Now that I understand the parts of this word, in what other words do these parts appear?

- • By analyzing the parts of vocabulary terms, I can predict the meaning of new words and relate new words to those I already know (by comparing and contrasting).

LEARNING NEW IDEAS IN AN EASY-TO-UNDERSTAND CONTEXT

- ❓ How can I use this new word or concept in conversation?
- ❓ How can I define this idea in my own words?

- • I can summarize new vocabulary and concepts in my own words and also use new vocabulary in context.

STAYING FOCUSED AND ALERT WHILE I AM LEARNING

- ❓ Am I staying focused on the task at hand?
- ❓ Should I shift my attention to another learning strategy for a while?
- ❓ Do I need a quick mental break?
- ❓ Would a break actually be worse for my focus right now?

- ❓ How can I stimulate my senses to maximize alertness while learning?

- • I employ strategies to keep myself mentally alert and focused when learning.

RETAINING (REMEMBERING) MY NEW KNOWLEDGE AND SKILLS

- ❓ What have I learned recently?
- ❓ What should I remember from recent lessons?
- ❓ What can I do to review what I have learned?
- ❓ What word play, pun, picture, acronym, simile, metaphor, mnemonic device, or other memory strategy will help me remember this new word or idea?
- ❓ Which memory strategies seem to work best for me?
- ❓ When will I get my studying done?
- ❓ How can I make time to study a little of each topic each day, rather than waiting until later?
- ❓ How will I manage my time while studying?
- ❓ What elements create a positive learning environment for me?

- ❓ What strategies will help me study effectively?
- ❓ How can I stay on task while studying?
- ❓ What tasks will I possibly need to perform by using my new knowledge or skills? (What questions might a teacher ask me?)
- ❓ Am I backtracking to review when I study so that I don't forget earlier concepts?

- • I employ the strategies that suit my needs for studying, remembering new concepts, and reviewing.
- • I find effective ways to remember new concepts in the short term and long term.

15 TAKING PERSONAL RESPONSIBILITY FOR MY LEARNING

- What are my personal responsibilities as a student, a worker, and a citizen?
- In what ways am I empowered to learn and grow?

- I can and will learn.

- I take personal responsibility for doing what it takes to succeed.
- I have a great support network, but my actions are the biggest key to my success.

16 SETTING LEARNING GOALS AND MONITORING MY PROGRESS

- What are my current career and life goals?
- What are my strengths and weaknesses?
- What knowledge and skills do I need to be successful in current and future situations?
- What do I need to learn to stay on the cutting edge?
- What new knowledge and skills would make me indispensable as a worker?
- What are my learning goals?

- How, where, and with what resources will I learn?
- How am I progressing toward my learning goals?
- Is my current learning strategy the best for achieving my goals?

- I know what short-term and long-term goals I want to achieve, and I can see my progress in reaching these goals.

17 ENGAGING IN A MINDSET[16] THAT LEADS TO SUCCESS

- How can I grow and develop my abilities today?
- What exciting challenges can I tackle today?
- How can I learn from this setback?
- What are my strengths and weaknesses, and how can I improve my weaknesses?

- Through effort, my abilities can be grown over time.
- My mind develops with every challenge I embrace, even if I do not always succeed.
- I will encounter setbacks, and I can use them to learn and grow.

WHERE do I stand in my development?	For each strategy (★) of this topic, where do I stand along the following range lines?	
Never Sometimes Often	Beginning Proficient Advanced	
Frequency I use each strategy, ask myself its Personal Empowerment Questions (PEQs), and affirm its Personal Empowerment Statements (PESs)	Current level of success in using each strategy, answering its Personal Empowerment Questions (PEQs), and affirming its Personal Empowerment Statements (PESs)	

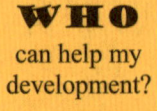

WHO can help my development?	• In addition to using the range lines above for self-assessment, I can ask others (parents, teachers, mentors, and peers) to assess me so that I can learn and grow from their observations and input. • I can observe the ways in which other people approach the skills I want to learn. What do other people do well? What do they need to improve? How can I use their example to improve myself? • I can talk to other people about how they approach the skills I want to develop. I can ask what strategies they use to be successful.

---

[16] (Dweck, 2007, pages 6, 7, 8, 10, 16, 17, 36, 57, 71, 72, and 167)

Leading and Motivating Others

WHY do I need this skill?	Leadership can take on many forms in school, professional, and personal life. Sometimes people assume roles as official leaders and at other times people lead by example to show others the way. *I should develop leadership and motivational skills so that I can assume leadership roles when my professional or personal life demands it.*
HOW will I develop this skill?	The same skills that are addressed earlier in this book can be used for leadership and motivation. Below, there are some strategies (★) for using these skills in a leadership role. To help myself use these strategies, I will *ask* myself the ❓ Personal Empowerment Questions (PEQs) below.

★ **In school, the workplace, and everyday life, I will use the strategies below.**
❓ **I will ask Personal Empowerment Questions (PEQs) like those below.**

1 DEVELOPING CONNECTIONS AS A LEADER

- ❓ What leadership roles might I have in the future?
- ❓ How can I learn about leadership from mentors and leaders like my teachers and parents (with whom I have connections)?
- ❓ How can I connect my team to our working environment in order to motivate them and maximize their work experience and effort?
- ❓ How can I promote peer connections in order to motivate my team, promote teamwork, and maximize their work experience and effort?

- ❓ How can I promote team spirit in order to motivate my team, promote teamwork, and maximize their work experience and effort?
- ❓ How can I develop motivating connections between my team and the community and world?

2 USING CRITICAL THINKING AND ASSESSMENT SKILLS AS A LEADER

- ❓ How well is this team, performance, system, process, or structure working?

- ❓ What needs to be and can be improved?
- ❓ What level of motivation does my team have?

3 PROBLEM SOLVING AND TAKING ACTION AS A LEADER

- ❓ How can I lead others in improving our team, performances, systems, processes, and structures?

- ❓ How can I motivate my team to take action?

4 BEING CREATIVE AS A LEADER

- ❓ How can I infuse creativity into my leadership actions?
- ❓ How can I use my resources to do something new?
- ❓ What new methods can we use to accomplish our goals?

- ❓ What new goals can we set out to achieve?
- ❓ How can I motivate in a creative way?

71

UNDERSTANDING AND INTERACTING WITH OTHERS AS A LEADER

❓ What are the needs, wants, and motivations of my teammates?

❓ How can I effectively communicate with my team?

❓ How can I improve collaboration among my team members?

❓ How can I motivate my team?

❓ How do other leaders motivate their teams, communicate effectively, and show charisma?

❓ How can I build connections among my teammates?

❓ How can I show respect for and confidence in my team?

❓ How can I make my teammates feel validated and appreciated?

❓ How can I prepare my team for competition?

USING QUALITY PERSONAL SKILLS, ATTITUDES, AND HABITS AS A LEADER

❓ How do I use, display, and promote a quality work ethic, adaptability, a competitive edge, a calm demeanor, organization, efficiency, a motivated attitude, ethical behavior, competent risk assessment, and financial literacy?

❓ What goals can our team create?

USING TECHNOLOGY AND INFORMATION AS A LEADER

❓ What technologies and information will allow me to better lead?

❓ How can technology help my team function better to accomplish its goals?

❓ What information and technology will allow me to motivate my team?

LEARNING AS A LEADER

❓ What can I learn to improve as a leader and motivator?

❓ What do my experiences as a leader and motivator teach me about handling future leadership situations?

WHERE do I stand in my development?	For each strategy (★) of this topic, where do I stand along the following range lines?	
Never Sometimes Often	Beginning Proficient Advanced	
Frequency I use each strategy and ask myself its Personal Empowerment Questions (PEQs)	Current level of success in using each strategy and answering its Personal Empowerment Questions (PEQs)	

WHO can help my development?	• In addition to using the range lines above for self-assessment, I can ask others (parents, teachers, mentors, and peers) to assess me so that I can learn and grow from their observations and input. • I can observe the ways in which other people approach the skills I want to learn. What do other people do well? What do they need to improve? How can I use their example to improve myself? • I can talk to other people about how they approach the skills I want to develop. I can ask what strategies they use to be successful.

Leading and Motivating Others

Bibliography

The World Factbook - Country Comparison: Population. (2012, July est.). Retrieved from Central Intelligence Agency: https://www.cia.gov/library/publications/the-world-factbook/rankorder/2119rank.html

Anderson, L. & Krathwohl, D. (2001). *A Taxonomy for Learning, Teaching, and Assessing: A Revision of Bloom's Taxonomy of Educational Objectives.* New York: Addison Wesley Longman, Inc.

Bergin, C. & Bergin, D. (2009, June). Attachment in the Classroom. *Educational Psychology Review, 21,* 141-170. Retrieved from Springer: http://rd.springer.com/article/10.1007/s10648-009-9104-0#

Casner-Lotto, J., Barrington, L., & Wright, M. (2006, Oct). *Are They Really Ready To Work: Employers' Perspectives on the Basic Knowledge and Applied Skills of New Entrants to the 21st Century U.S. Workforce.* Retrieved from The Partnership for 21st Century Skills: http://www.p21.org/storage/documents/FINAL_REPORT_PDF09-29-06.pdf

Dweck, C. (2007). *Mindset: The New Psychology of Success.* New York: Ballantine Books.

Eberle, B. (1996). *Scamper: Games for Imagination Development.* Waco, TX: Prufrock Press, Inc.

ETR Associates. *What is Service-Learning?* Retrieved from National Service-Learning Clearinghouse: http://www.servicelearning.org/what-service-learning

Friedman, T. (2005). *The World is Flat: A Brief History of the Twenty-first Century.* New York: Farrar, Straus and Giroux.

As of the publication of this book in 2012, all webpage links were active.